2.a

THE NATIONAL COUNCIL FOR CIVIL LIBERTIES

THE NATIONAL COUNCIL FOR CIVIL LIBERTIES

The First Fifty Years

Mark Lilly

MACMILLAN

First published 1984 by
THE MACMILLAN PRESS LTD
London and Basingstoke
Companies and representatives
throughout the world

Typeset by
Wessex Typesetters Ltd
Frome, Somerset

Printed in Great Britain by
The Pitman Press, Bath

British Library Cataloguing in Publication Data
Lilly, Mark
The National Council for Civil Liberties.
1. National Council for Civil Liberties—History
I. Title
323.4'06'041   JC599.G7
ISBN 0–333–36974–2
ISBN 0–333–36975–0 Pbk

For Davey

Contents

Preface

The National Council for Civil Liberties was founded 50 years ago in 1934. The aim of this book is to describe some of the issues, and the related campaigns, over that period, and to show the diversity of the Council's work, and its changing role.

No attempt has been made to give a comprehensive account of every campaign and every libertarian issue. Rather, I have used a selective focus to highlight very specific areas of interest in order to be able to go into them in greater depth. The book is arranged on a chronological as well as a thematic basis, so that the reader will have a sense of a developing story. Each chapter is defined by a period of years, but I have not hesitated to go outside these dates if it is necessary in the interests of clarity.

Because of the nature of the book, it has inevitably been the case that many distinguished and dedicated civil libertarians, both within NCCL and outside it, have been mentioned only in passing, or not at all. Although they are not the sort of people who would seek public recognition for their work, I nevertheless regret that it has not been possible to acknowledge all of their contributions to the continuing fight for a freer society.

Acknowledgements

In writing this book I have been exceptionally lucky in being able to draw heavily on the expertise of colleagues associated with the Council. Some of the material in the first two chapters is based on the unpublished autobiography of Sylvia Scaffardi, who has not only allowed me to make free use of that source but has contributed valuable amendments to my original draft. Melissa Benn, Jean Rogers and Cash Scorer did a great deal of work for the final chapters. Linda Gage, Jean Rogers and, above all, Roger Cornwell read the complete manuscript and made innumerable useful suggestions for change. Malcolm Hurwitt, the Secretary of the Cobden Trust and a long-standing member of the executive committee, and Professor John Saville, of the Campaign for Academic Freedom and Democracy, have both kindly contributed appendices on their organisations. My warmest thanks to these kind helpers.

I am grateful to the publishing house of Edward Arnold for permission to quote from E. M. Forster's *Two Cheers for Democracy*.

1 1934–39

THE FORMATION OF NCCL

On a cold evening on 1 November 1932, while the hunger marchers were streaming towards Parliament Square for the climax of their campaign in London, after three hard weeks on the road, the evening papers placarded the news that Wal Hannington, their leader, had been arrested and refused bail. The charge against him was that of attempting to disaffect the police by appealing to their sense of working class solidarity; they too should join in resisting the economic measures that affected them all.

Dense crowds were thronging Westminster and the traffic was halted. The marchers had brought with them a million signatures on a petition against the 10 per cent cuts in unemployment benefit and the means test. They and their followers had struggled and fought their way against police cordons and baton charges, trying to carry the petition down Whitehall to Parliament. They were unaware that when the deputation of fifty had arrived at Charing Cross it had been surrounded by police and the petition confiscated.

A one-time freelance journalist, who had been following the demonstration all evening, found himself at about 9.30 at the junction of Trafalgar Square and Whitehall. It was during a lull that his attention was attracted to two men in cloth caps, heavy boots, and mufflers. They were actively inciting the crowd to advance towards the police cordon which had closed off Whitehall near the War Office. There was little response from the crowd, but a certain amount of pushing and shoving.

He crossed over to get nearer the action, and saw the men draw regulation police truncheons from their hip pockets and make two arrests. As they marched their men off, the cordon on Whitehall parted to let them through.

The observer was Ronald Kidd. The police use of *agents-provocateurs*, which he saw and recorded that night, was the central motive in his setting up the National Council for Civil Liberties.

At the time, he was running the 'Punch and Judy' bookshop in no more than a cubby-hole in Villiers Street off the Strand. If you wanted to read an unexpurgated copy of D. H. Lawrence's *Lady Chatterley's Lover*, or Radclyffe Hall's *The Well of Loneliness*, or a book about the USSR which was not full of hysterical anti-communism, you could call in there. It became a place of friendly chat with a radical flavour. Kidd had previously worked at a wide variety of jobs; as well as journalism, he had tried advertising, freelance work for publishers, theatrical stage management and even the occasional acting. One of his unfinished projects was an account of some of London's attractive old buildings threatened with demolition.

The bookshop yielded no more than pocket money; the publishing company he got involved in a little later was even worse – he was cheated by a partner. These commercial failures probably reflected his lack of interest in the whole money ethos. His energies were directed elsewhere.

1933 was a black year for civil liberties. As Sylvia Scaffardi recalls:

> The British public relaxed in the universal popular resort of the cinema (in the slow days of the 1930s, before television and before instant communication), listened to the bland voice of British Movietone News telling them that Hindenberg had invited Hitler to become Chancellor of Germany, and that Hitler was 'guiding Germany back to peaceful progress'. The young storm-troopers keeping order in the streets outside placarded shops were his loyal followers.
>
> In another newsreel, Sir Oswald Mosley appears, theat-

rically plugging British fascism (The *Daily Mail* is backing him – 'Hurrah for the Blackshirts'). 'We do not propose a dictatorship,' he enunciated, 'but a dramatic revision of the Parliamentary machine, a fight for action, for vigorous vitality and manhood, against the forces of drift and despair.'

An independent documentary film made by Ivor Montagu on the German leader Ernst Thalmann was censored by Lord Tyrrell, the Chairman of the British Board of Film Censors. Thalmann, who led a sizeable representation of Communist members in the German Parliament, was imprisoned without charge or trial one month after Hitler came to power. Lord Tyrrell explained that films about criminals were not allowed.[1]

This was the climate that gave birth to NCCL and assured it at once of influential support. The starting point was a lively correspondence in the *Week-End Review* arising out of an article by A. P. Herbert (on 5 August 1933) denouncing the use of plain-clothes policemen to infiltrate night clubs and order drinks after hours so as to get convictions. Herbert complained that the liberty of the subject was no longer held sacred, Parliament was indifferent, and so on.

So much moral indignation for so trivial a cause stuck in the gullet of Ronald Kidd, who challenged Herbert to protest at the use of police *agents-provocateurs*, not against after-hours drinkers, but against hunger marchers. Herbert has the grace to agree to pursue the matter with the Commissioner of the Metropolitan Police, Lord Trenchard, provided that Kidd could furnish some evidence for his charges. On his way to swear an affidavit, Kidd, by great good luck, bumped into a journalist friend who had also covered that hunger march, and could offer similar evidence to support his own affidavit.

True to his word, Herbert took the case up with Trenchard, and the latter's flimsy attempts at denial were described by Herbert in a piece which appeared in the October 28 edition of the *Review* under the title 'Mr Kidd and the Agent-Provocateur'. Whilst denying that police had acted as *agents-*

provocateurs, Trenchard had committed himself to saying that if they were to do so, then they could expect to be dealt with severely. Kidd was delighted with this statement; through his own efforts he had been instrumental in engineering Trenchard into the desired position. It was the optimism generated by this success, combined with a passionate concern for civil liberties, which provided the impetus for the setting up of NCCL.

Kidd's idea was that if he could bring together a number of eminent writers, journalists, lawyers, and MPs, and persuade them to act as observers during mass gatherings – he had especially in mind the arrival in London of the 1934 Hunger March – then the complaints about police harassment which hitherto had gone largely uncredited (because they came predominantly from the victims themselves) would be widely believed.

This plan was later widened – since so many vital issues were cropping up in addition to the hunger march – so that what was envisaged was a permanent watchdog body operating not only as observers, but also through Parliament, public meetings, the press, and the Courts. It would have its own publications, meetings, and demonstrations.

Kidd's companion in this enterprise, as in his private life, was Sylvia Crowther-Smith (now Sylvia Scaffardi). They had met six years earlier when he was stage-managing in a provincial repertory company. Their room, at 3 Dansey Place, in Soho, was to become the Council's first office.

The inaugural meeting was held on 22 February 1934, in a little half-basement room in St Martin-in-the-Fields Church in Trafalgar Square. About twenty people were present, including Dr Edith Summerskill, Anabel Williams-Ellis, Mrs Haden-Guest, Kingsley Martin, Claud Cockburn, two young barristers (Dudley Coppard and Geoffrey Bing), two solicitors (David Freeman and Ambrose Appelbe), Alun Thomas of the International Labour Defence, Professor Catlin (husband to Vera Brittain), Professor W. E. Le Gros Clark, and the writer Douglas Goldring.

Sylvia Scaffardi gives a brief account of the meeting, at which she was present. Kidd agreed to take on the role of secretary, and an executive of twenty-four members was to be formed which would meet monthly. It was decided to approach either Henry Nevinson or E. M. Forster to act as president; someone, at any rate, not party political, who would encourage others from all sections of political opinion to lend the Council support. There was agreement that the first priority was to set up a vigilance committee to observe the arrival of the hunger marchers three days later, on Sunday, 25 February. There were, of course, speeches: 'They were all in sympathy, a free press, freedom of association, democratic control of government – the cliches of liberty – no longer to be taken for granted . . . Professor W. E. Le Gros Clark . . . spoke with passion of the ground trembling under out feet.'[2]

Kidd clearly had an extraordinary ability to secure the support of major figures in public life, as can be seen from the list of vice-presidents.[3] Some of these, including H. G. Wells, agreed to act as observers in Hyde Park on the 25 February to keep an eye on police behaviour. There was some expectation that London was about to see a repetition of the ugly scenes of violence that attended the earlier march of 1932. The current situation was not helped by the attitude of the Home Secretary, Sir John Gilmour, who was clearly trying to deflect criticism of the government's record. He tried to discredit the march by emphasising that the organising body, the National Unemployed Workers' Movement, was run by communists (which it was) and that the arrival of the marchers would lead to serious disorder. In a notorious statement, he warned parents to make sure their children were off the streets and that people should put themselves safely behind closed doors. Similarly, the police advised shopkeepers to put up their shutters to avoid having their windows broken.

The events immediately preceding the Hyde Park rally showed the determination of the authorities to prevent the NUWM gaining a success. Wal Hannington gives an account of how the police tried to prevent him, a few days before the rally, from attending a meeting at the House of Commons to which he had been invited; the Speaker had apparently banned him from the House because of disturbances in which he had been involved on an earlier occasion. As he stood outside, his way barred, sympathetic MPs explained how he could get in surreptitiously through a tunnel private to MPs which ran from Westminster underground station straight into the House. He walked through, head down as though in meditation. The police, seeing a vaguely familiar figure, saluted him with the words 'Good night, Sir', to which he replied 'Good night, officer.' By this means, he was able to attend the whole meeting without further difficulties, and astonished the police outside when he emerged after it.[4]

On 22 February, five of the hunger marchers from the Tyneside contingent were arrested and charged with 'wife desertion': the pretext for bringing the charge was that the wives in question were claiming poor relief during their husbands' absence. The prosecution was unsuccessful. (Even after the march, seven men from Fife were arrested on a similar charge. The Dunfermline sheriff's court also threw out the case, 'and the men were acquitted amidst applause in the public gallery'.)[5]

On the 23 February, two of the organisers, Tom Mann and Harry Pollitt, were arrested and accused of having made seditious speeches in the Rhondda the previous weekend. There was such a public outcry at this blatant use of the judicial process to harass political opponents that when the two men appeared in court at Pontypridd, they were both released on bail.

On the 24 February, the *Manchester Guardian* and *The Times* printed a letter from Kidd and fourteen others, announcing the formation of the Council:

The present hunger march has been preceded by public statements by the Home Secretary and the Attorney General (who has already hinted at the possibility of bloodshed) which we feel justify apprehension. Furthermore, certain features of the police preparations for the present march – for example, instructions to shopkeepers to barricade their windows – cannot but create an atmosphere of misgiving, not only dangerous but unjustified by the facts.

All reports bear witness to the excellent discipline of the marchers. From their own leaders they have received repeated instructions of the strictest character, warning them against any breach of the peace, even under extreme provocation.

In view of the general and alarming tendency to encroach on the liberty of the citizen, there has recently been formed a Council for Civil Liberties. One of the special duties of this Council will be to maintain a vigilant observation of the proceedings of the next few days. Relevant and well authenticated reports by responsible persons will be welcomed and investigated by the council.[6]

On the Sunday itself, Kidd was nervous lest some of the distinguished observers should fail to turn up. Claud Cockburn was deputed to go and fetch H. G. Wells. He dragged him away from his lunch, and brought him to the park where, in the company of the other observers, they strolled across the expanse of grass separating the mounted police from the speakers' platforms.

Suddenly Mr Wells dug his umbrella into the mud and said 'I refuse to go any farther. I detect' he said, turning to me, 'your plan. At any moment now, as a result of some prearranged signal on your part, the situation will get out of hand, the police will charge, a dozen prominent authors and legislators will be bourne to the ground, and you will have the incident you desire.' Just at that moment it looked to me like quite an idea, and I was sorry I hadn't thought of it earlier.[7]

In fact, despite all the anxiety and trepidation manufactured by the National Government, the whole demonstration was entirely peaceful. Music from the fifes, drums, and bagpipes of the Scottish marchers filled the park. Packets of cigarettes were thrown through the air as presents for the Welsh contingent. The *Internationale* was sung. A chief focus of the march was to protest against the 10 per cent cut in unemployment relief, and within a few weeks Neville Chamberlain had given in and rescinded the cut. In the whole affair, the greatest bitterness was directed against the Prime Minister, Ramsay Macdonald. He had been Labour Prime Minister in 1924, and again in 1929, but with the depression, he agreed in 1931 to head a National Government which was predominantly Conservative. This desertion was bad enough, but when the march organisers asked that the Cabinet should meet their delegation, his refusal was couched in the most offensive terms. In the first instance Macdonald did not even send a personal reply, but gave his private secretary, J. A. Barlow, the task of writing to the march leaders. The tone was crisp: 'I have been instructed by the Prime Minister to say that it is impossible to accede to your request. The deputation can do no service to the unemployed. The communist purpose of these marches is common knowledge.'[8] Some days later, the Commons spent a considerable time debating the issue, but despite widespread support for the meeting from many MPs, Macdonald remained dismissive: 'has anybody who cares to come to London, either on foot or in first-class carriages, the constitutional right to demand to see me, to take up my time, whether I like it or not? I say he has nothing of the kind. If they think they have a constitutional right to compel me to see them, they are very much mistaken'. As an evening newspaper, the *Star*, wryly remarked, far more of his own time was taken up in refusing to hold the meeting than would have been taken up in holding it.[9]

I have dwelt on the 1932 and 1934 marches not only because they were the events around which the Council was formed, but also because much of what happened can be seen as characteristic of so many of the causes the NCCL was to espouse in the next fifty years. There was a major and justified grievance; the authorities sought to direct attention away from that grievance by emphasising supposedly sinister influences behind the agitation (in this case, the Communists), and by the manufacture of alarm about public disorder. In the 1932 march (though clearly not in 1934) the police used *agents-provocateurs* actually to bring about the very disorder which they had warned the general public the marchers might cause; the law was being used to bring absurd charges (sedition, wife desertion) not so much in the hope of conviction, but as a form of harassment; and finally, government ministers callously disregarded the issues themselves, and seemed interested only in bureaucratic regulation, face-saving, and using their privileged access to publicity to hold up their weaker opponents to derision.

In the event, the flat near Selfridges that had been volunteered as a sort of operation room for NCCL observers, was never used. No telephone reports of baton charges, bleeding heads, or smashed windows, ever came through. Writing in 1940, Kidd comments on the outcome: 'Events proved that the Home Secretary was mistaken. There was no bloodshed and no disorder. The march passed off perfectly quietly. Since then, other Hunger Marchers have come to London and used their age-old right to demonstrate on an empty stomach, and citizens in London have been made aware of the acute problems of the industrial and distressed areas.'[10]

The fledgling NCCL had now to consolidate its position and move on the broader aims that had already been identified. Kidd became General Secretary and Sylvia Crowther-Smith Assistant Secretary. Their room doubled as NCCL's headquarters. Access was through an open entrance and up steep metal stairs to a single bare-boarded room, half of it partitioned off as their living quarters, and the other half serving as the Council's office. It was here that E. M. Forster, then 55 and an eminent man of letters, came to meet Kidd, who had invited him to accept the presidency of the Council.

But there were other disadvantages to Dansey Place as an office. Once, the press of people wanting to get in was so great that part of the staircase gave way. As soon as it could, NCCL moved to a suite of three rooms in the Charing Cross Road – approached by a flight of stone steps.

FASCISM

In 1932, two years before the formation of the Council, Oswald Mosley had founded the British Union of Fascists, in more or less direct imitation of Mussolini's Blackshirts. The rise of the BUF, and in particular the nature of its rallies and demonstrations, was to figure largely in the history of the mid-1930s.

NCCL's concerns were threefold. In the first place, it was horrified at the anti-Semitism which was at the core of the BUF's popular appeal. Secondly, the police partiality in favour of the BUF and against the anti-Fascists, was seen as of a piece with their treatment of striking workers, campaigners against the 'Sedition Bill', hunger marchers and the unemployed holding public meetings to air their grievances. Those charged with the task of protecting and serving all classes and groups in society disinterestedly, acted like authoritarian vigilantes defending ruling class interests against everyone else. The third concern was with the legislative consequence of the disorder which the BUF had created both in halls and on the streets: the Public Order Act of 1936.

Most of NCCL's energies were channelled into the debate about the mass rallies and meetings. The first and most notorious of these was the Blackshirt rally held in London, at Olympia, on 7 June 1934. Anti-Fascist hecklers inside the meeting were set upon by Blackshirt stewards and in many cases savagely beaten up before being ejected. The violence itself was bad enough, but what provoked the greatest controversy was the refusal of the police, who were outside the hall, to intervene. Under strenuous questioning in the Commons, the Home Secretary, Sir John Gilmour, stated that it was his view that the police did not have any legal right to enter the hall uninvited unless they suspected that a breach of the peace was occurring. One would have thought that injured hecklers ejected from the meeting and conspicuous to all outside the hall (including, of course, the police) would have constituted sufficient grounds for suspecting such a breach.

Nevertheless, Gilmour's account of the legal position with regard to police presence at indoor meetings of this kind was unassailable; until, that is, the decision in *Thomas v Sawkins* changed the position radically. Alun Thomas was due to speak at a public meeting in the library at Caerau in Glamorgan on 17 August 1934, against the 'Sedition Bill'. Several policemen, amongst them Sergeant Sawkins, insisted on being present at this meeting despite repeated requests to leave. There was even a vote taken which was almost unanimous in supporting Thomas' desire that the police leave. In the end, Thomas made as if to eject one of the policemen. As the law was then understood, if there were no question of a breach of the peace taking place, the police's insistence on remaining after being asked to leave constituted an act of trespass, and Thomas was entitled to use reasonable force to throw them out. Sergeant Sawkins intervened once Thomas had laid hands on his colleague and it was this intervention that Thomas took up with the courts. He brought an action against Sawkins for assault, which was dismissed by the magistrates. NCCL, realising the important repercussions if this decision were left to stand, briefed Stafford Cripps and Dingle Foot, and they duly appeared for Thomas at the appeal held in the Divisional Court in May 1935. The ruling was that the right of the police to enter a meeting was not limited to cases where there was a breach of the peace, or even where such a breach was reasonably suspected, but embraced all cases in which the police believed that any offence of any kind at all was likely to be committed. Writing in 1975, Cox could say that the police 'have rarely used this power'[11] but Kidd, in 1940, was seriously alarmed:

I venture, temperately and with great respect, to submit that in the *Thomas v Sawkins* appeal the judgement was not, in fact, a clarification or explanation of the law as it had existed from time immemorial, but that it enunciated a new and unheard-of principle in British law. . . . Never, I believe, at any time in legal history has it been held sufficient (in order to justify such entry) that police may constitute themselves prophets in this way . . . [the] decision was wrong in law and disastrous to our civil rights.[12]

It shows very clearly that the attitude of the police towards public meetings varied according to the politics of the participants. In Glamorgan, they were determined to sniff out sedition from the left-wing; at Olympia, on the other hand, they allowed Mosley a free hand.

The anti-Semitic nature of many of the BUF meetings inevitably led to physical attacks against Jews. During a Commons' debate on 10 July 1936, Mr R. W. Sorensen (Labour) gave details of some of these meetings:

The Blackshirt speaker said that the Jews maintained that the child of a Christian marriage was no better than an animal, quoting a supposed saying from the Talmud; that Jews were brought up to believe that all Christians were illegitimate and that in the Jewish Kol Nidre service it was stated that Jews had perfect freedom to swindle and rob Christians. At other Blackshirt meetings the observers of the National Council [for Civil Liberties] took notes of anti-Semitic provocation, one notorious Blackshirt speaker reeling off a long list of surnames of prominent living Jewish men, describing them as 'hook-nosed, yellow-skinned, dirty Jewish swine'. At another meeting the speaker described the Jews as 'venereal-ridden vagrants'.[13]

Jewish shopkeepers had their premises damaged with frightening regularity. One newspaper reporter counted more than twenty smashed shop windows on one evening along Bethnal Green Road, Green Street, Globe Road and the immediate vicinity; he also saw hundreds of chalked anti-Jewish slogans on the walls of private houses and shops, and on the synagogue in Green Street.

The attack on the Jewish community in the East End was, of course, a matter which NCCL took to heart. What gave the matter added urgency was the attitude of the police. All too frequently they turned a blind eye to the activities of the bullies. This is typical of the signed statements handed to NCCL:

I was distributing copies of the 'Citizen' for the Bethnal Green Labour Party on Monday evening, February 22nd, at 9 pm in Norton Street, Bethnal Green, accompanied by one other literature distributor. We were putting copies of the paper under doors. A number of young men, aged between twenty and twenty-five, came down the street shouting Fascist slogans and singing songs. They saw me and came over. One asked me what I was doing, snatched the papers out of my hands and then they attacked me. I was thrown to the ground, kicked on my body and ankles. I managed to get up and run. I immediately reported this at the Bethnal Green Police Station. The officer in charge took particulars, but I heard no more.[14]

In this instance it is of course possible that the police did their best to find the culprits and were simply unlucky. However, as more and more complainants found that they too 'heard no more', less generous inferences must be made about the police.

The extent of the anti-Semitism generated by Mosley's Blackshirts can be gauged by reading the very first edition of the Council's paper, *Civil Liberty*. Details are given of scores of cases in which individual Jews, mostly from the East End, were physically attacked or had their property damaged. Magistrates were notoriously lenient. Here is an account of a case heard in a North London Police Court: 'A law-abiding Jewish citizen had been cruelly beaten up by a young Blackshirt. He was removed to hopsital and detained. Two doctors gave evidence that the wounds were caused by a metal bar or other sharp instruments. For thus causing grievous bodily harm the young Blackshirt was bound over by the Magistrate.'[15]

The violence, both on the streets and at indoor meetings, which had been generated by Fascism and anti-Fascism, led a frightened Parliament to pass the Public Order Act of 1936. The main provision, and one which had been drafted with Mosley's Blackshirts specifically in mind, made it an offence to wear political uniform in public. Whilst the Council was happy with this clause, it was alarmed at the change in the way that demonstrations could be banned. Before the Act, there were essentially two methods open to the authorities if they wished to interfere. Either the police could insist on regulating the route of any procession, under powers contained in the Metropolitan Police Act 1839. Alternatively, the police could effectively prevent a procession by applying to the magistrates to have the organisers bound over to keep the peace. Under the new Act, the police could place the ban themselves, without having to consult magistrates, as long as they had reasonable grounds for fearing serious public disorder. The Council felt that this formula was insufficiently tight to prevent bans being placed in an arbitrary fashion.

In the event, they were to discover that the police, once they had been alerted to the dangers of one particular set of marchers, adopted the habit of banning all marches of whatever kind. For example, Mosley's threat to march through the East End in July 1937 led to one of these blanket bans. This effectively meant that the police were regularly able to suspend one of the basic freedoms – the freedom of assembly – under the guise of preventing disorder. There were no legal difficulties in preventing specific demonstrations; indeed, the authorities had fully three options. They could use common law powers to bind over the organisers to keep the peace, as was established in *Wise* v *Dunning* (1902). They could invoke section 3(1) of the new Act, which gave police the power to prevent a procession from entering specific areas; an especially effective move if the purpose of the demonstration was to provoke and insult specific communities (as it always was when the Blackshirts marched through the East End). Finally, under section 3(3) of the Public Order Act, they could ban certain classes of procession. The use of blanket bans was, therefore, quite unwarranted, and it was employed to stifle dissent and to suit the convenience of the authorities. The situation in the 1970s and 80s, with the various proposed marches of the National Front and other Fascist organisations, and the blanket bans which result, shows how little has changed in half a century.

Section 5 of the Public Order Act deals with threatening or insulting words and behaviour. This had already been an offence, of course, but the Act dramatically increased the maximum fine (from £2 to £50) and generally widened the scope of the application of the offence. In July 1937, two prosecutions came to the notice of the NCCL. In the first, a man on his way home came across a Fascist meeting at Stepney Green and whistled at it. He was charged under section 5. The magistrate dismissed the case, saying: 'I think it would be a sad state of affairs if it were a criminal offence for some irresponsible young man to put his fingers to his mouth and whistle. I don't regard that as conduct which ought to fall within the scope of this particular section of the Act.'[16] The second case was even more risible. Another man approached the same crowd, 'and blew his nose in a manner which apparently offended the inspector, who immediately ordered his arrest'.[17] This case was also thrown out. Although both cases appear comic as we read them today, it is as well to remember that they both show how harassment can be based on the feeblest legal pretext (as we saw earlier with the charges of wife desertion brought against some of the hunger marchers); and once again we note that both defendants happened to be in the anti-Fascist camp.

The remarkable tenacity of D. N. Pritt in the cause of civil liberties, and the contrast of the fudging evasions of the Home Secretary, are marvellously illustrated in the former's auto-biography, when he deals with section 6 of the Public Order Act. Under this section, a police officer is entitled to take the name and address of a heckler at a public meeting if s/he is reasonably suspected of committing an offence under the Act *and* if the chairperson of the meeting has requested that the police take this action. It came to Pritt's notice in 1947 that members of South Kensington Labour Party were heckling at Fascist meetings and the police were taking their names and addresses *and handing them to the chairperson*!

Pritt asked a question in the House about this, and was told by the Home Secretary that 'a name and address may be given to the Chairman in a case in which the police do not intend to institute proceedings, so that those responsible for organising the meeting may prosecute if they so wish'.[18] Although the giving of these details to chairpersons was not illegal, Pritt saw it, quite rightly, as grossly improper, especially as it rendered the hecklers liable to reprisals from the Fascist organisers of the meeting. He worried away at the Home Secretary, Chuter Ede, who, nevertheless, refused to concede the point. Pritt wrote a piece for the *New Statesman*. Ede replied, making reference to the debate in Parliament on the Public Order Act. Pritt dismissed this with magisterial contempt in yet another *Statesman* letter: 'It is of course elementary that what was said in debate cannot be taken into consideration – cannot indeed even be mentioned – in interpreting statutes . . .'.[19] We should not be too surprised to find, however, that at the end of the day, Ede, without the slightest justification, was sticking to his guns.

In the same year in which the Public Order Act was passed, a particularly notorious example of police partiality was seen in the circumstances surrounding the Thurloe Square disturbances of 22 March 1936. An anti-Fascist meeting was being held in the square at the same time as a Blackshirt rally was being held in the Albert Hall nearby. The speakers were not only arguing against Fascist doctrines but against the policy of the Albert Hall management in letting their premises to the Blackshirts but not to their opponents. The meeting started at about 8.00 pm and at 9.00 pm police on horseback advanced without warning, and rode their horses into the tightly packed crowd and started batoning right and left indiscriminately, injuring men and women. Groups of persons were forced against the railings and wedged there by the police horses and were then struck by police batons.[20] Three days later, D. N. Pritt and Dingle Foot in a special adjournment debate in the Commons, were relentlessly pressing Sir John Simon, the Home Secretary, for an official enquiry.

When this was refused, NCCL decided to go ahead with its own inquiry. The brutal nature of the baton charge aroused strong feelings, and the public was demanding an explanation. The quality of the witnesses led NCCL to believe that it could come up with one. It therefore appointed a Commission of Inquiry, to gather eye-witnesses' statements and publish findings which it was hoped would induce the Home Secretary to reverse his earlier decision not to hold an official inquiry.

The Commission had a membership of six, comprising two professors, a barrister, a Quaker business man, Eleanor Rathbone and J. B. Priestley. They received oral evidence from 31 witnesses, nine of whom were NCCL observers who had been present in Thurloe Square with the express intention of recording and reporting on events. They heard that the police had been present in Thurloe Square from the start, but had made no attempt to prevent the meeting from taking place, or to disperse the crowd, until the mounted police had arrived and attacked the crowd. There was a large body of evidence that the meeting was a peaceful one. No one had been arrested in the square, nor had any policeman been injured there, nor had any householder made a complaint against the meeting. The Commission concluded that the baton charge itself had been both unnecessary and unprovoked, and that the charges of police brutality were substantiated.

This lack of even-handedness in police behaviour had figured in the very first annual report of the Council: 'The big Fascist and Anti-Fascist demonstrations held in London and the provinces in September, October and November were the occasion of serious attempts at limiting or even prohibiting the right of assembly. On each occasion the facilities and protection given to uniformed Blackshirts were in sharp contrast to the attempts of the authorities to suppress anti-Fascist activities.'[21]

NCCL repeatedly and vigorously denounced this favouritism, with mixed success. For example, when the local Chief Constable attempted to ban an anti-Fascist demonstration in Manchester late in September 1934 (which had been organised to coincide with the Blackshirt rally at Bellevue), the Council sent letters and telegrams, obtained and published an eminent barrister's opinion that the purported ban was illegal, enlisted the aid of the Salford and Manchester Trades Council, sent a deputation to the Home Office, and generally whipped up the press in support. On the day, the police allowed the anti-Fascists their protest without interference. However, the same tactics failed in Liverpool; the Chief Constable insisted on his right to ban the proposed gathering, and when the anti-Fascists defied him, they were dispersed with a baton charge.

In January 1939, there were two demonstrations in London. The first, on the 14 January, was a Fascist protest against aid to refugees, including those attempting to flee from Nazi Germany. Scuffles broke out. The *Sunday Express* told how their photographer was '. . . attacked by a mob of hooligans as he attempted to take pictures of the crowd in Piccadilly Circus. . . . Here and there a few sang the Horst Wessel Nazi anthem, and threw anti-Jewish pamphlets about. They spotted Coote and his camera. Shouting 'Dirty Jew' – he is not a Jew – they made for him. He was knocked down and kicked several times in the stomach'.[22] The police, however, were loath to make any arrests. An eye-witness recalls:

I remained as an interested observer in the Circus for about an hour. . . . A number of other cases of assault and interference with members of the public took place within my hearing without any intervention on the part of the police, who could not have failed to be witnesses. I was, in fact, amazed at the apparent apathy of the police towards the demonstrators, especially in view of the fact that the latter were provocative and of a hooligan type. I was also very surprised that for a solid hour the police allowed the traffic in Piccadilly Circus to be disorganised at the peak hour. The crowd of demonstrators caused congestion but during this time the police took no steps at all to move them on in order to avoid obstruction.[23]

The second demonstration in London (on 31 January) was anti-Fascist. Its purpose was to call for arms to be supplied to the Spanish Republic against Franco's Nationalists. At about 9.30 in the evening a crowd of people who were waiting in Old Palace Yard to lobby members of Parliament were charged by mounted police from two directions. A man and woman attempting to escape the hubbub were dragged backwards off a bus by police. A café on the Embankment was raided by police in pursuit of over twenty of the crowd who had sought refuge there; four of them were dragged out and beaten. A witness in Parliament Square records: 'I saw an Inspector of Police violently kick an unsuspecting man with such force that he was sent sprawling into the roadway. Before he had time to get up he was set upon by three policemen in a brutal way.'[24] At about 11.00 pm that evening, there was another charge of mounted police, this time in Piccadilly Circus, where some of the crowd had gone.

The Council collected statements from reliable witnesses and held a meeting with interested MPs at the House of Commons. Sydney Silverman had faith in the statements and raised the matter in debate. It was clear, he said, 'that large numbers of people in this country believe that the demonstrators were unlawfully and violently prevented by the police from demonstrating in a cause which did not happen to be pleasing to the government of the day'.[25]

Thus, throughout the 1930s, Fascists were treated with indulgence under a dispensation which was based on the blind eye; whereas anti-Fascist events were systematically harassed. It is assuredly one of the most disgraceful episodes in the history of policing in the modern period.

'NON-FLAM' FILMS

The controversy surrounding 'non-flam' films provides an
early example of the tendency of the authorities to use existing
legislation to achieve aims quite alien to the intentions of the
original legislators.

In the early years of the century, there was considerable
public alarm about the safety of audiences watching celluloid
(or 'standard') films, because such films were highly inflammable. As a result, the Cinematograph Act was passed in 1909. It
provides powers for local authorities to issue licences to film
exhibitors and of course it was assumed that such licences
would be granted on the basis of whether the exhibitor's
premises were deemed safe.

In practice, as we might expect, the local authorities used
their power to deny licences to those exhibitors showing films of
which they did not approve. This led to the film trade itself, led
by the Cinematograph Exhibitors Association, setting up the
British Board of Film Censors in 1912. Their hope was that if
they introduced some sort of self-regulation and refused to
certificate films which might be thought sexually frank or
politically sensitive, then the films which they did pass would
be exempt from the local authorities' interference. And this is
more or less what happened. For although the BBFC did not
(and does not) have any legal standing as a censor, in practice
local authorities ensured that uncertificated films were not seen
in their areas. We might smile today at some of the films, many
of them educational, which were censored by the Board. They
included, for example *The Mystery of Life*, from which was ex-
punged a sequence showing the mating of snails, and another
depicting the fertilisation of sea-urchin eggs. But on the whole,
the story of the Board, at least until the advent of John
Trevelyan in 1958, was one of miserable complicity with
narrow-minded authorities. Herbert Wilcox's marvellous
Dawn (1928), a film about Edith Cavell, was banned by the

BBFC because government policy at the time was against offering any offence to Germany. Similarly, the new revolutionary Soviet cinema (one thinks, above all, of Eisenstein's *Battleship Potemkin* of 1925) was denied to the British Public.

Not quite denied. Many small film societies, schools, adult education colleges and the like, had managed to screen some of these uncertificated educational, political and 'art' films by procuring copies made of cellulose–acetate, which, unlike celluloid, is not inflammable. There was no question of their constituting a safety threat, and so falling within the intended scope of the 1909 Act. This was the position in 1934, the first year of NCCL, when the Home Office announced its intention of extending the 1909 Act to include these 'non-flam' films.

There was, one is pleased to record, an outcry. If the films were safe, why was the Home Office trying to bring them into the scope of an Act purporting to be concerned exclusively with safety? The *Manchester Guardian* gave generous space to the 'non-flam' enthusiasts. R. S. Read, the principal of a technical college in West Hartlepool, made these telling points:

> It has been proved beyond doubt by those who have used the 'non-flam' films that there is not the slightest risk from fire. In the event of one of these films catching fire it merely smoulders and, unless an effort is made to keep it alight, goes out. In fact any personal danger connected with the use of sub-standard films is infinitesimal compared with the risks in engineering, chemistry and physics classes.
>
> The film is most valuable in the teaching of many subjects, such as physics, engineering, geography, and history, and it has been used in the building for the last three years. The cultural value of geographical films is very great, and the records of school sports and outings, etc., are most interesting and instructive.[26]

Writing to the paper on the same day, Neville Scott's anger seemed to get in the way of his ability to succeed with metaphors; pressure was being applied, he suggested, from those in high places, 'to bring the tides of education, which are now being taken at the flood, to a standstill'.

What was the Home Office up to? Why should it have ventured to displease sensible and responsible educationalists? Well, we have already seen one answer: 'undesirable' films were slipping through the censorship net and the Home Office simply wanted to suppress even this small anomaly. The second reason was that the film trade itself has been lobbying for some time against the 'non-flam' films because they feared competition. It seemed almost like a deal; the industry, through the BBFC, censored material that the Home Office did not like, and in return the Home Office would squeeze out the 'non-flam' opposition so as to increase the exhibitors' profits.

The role that the NCCL played in the controversy was twofold; in the first place, it was quick to produce a pamphlet on the subject[27] and secondly, it was involved in court hearings. The first such case arose out of a film show held at the Miners' Hall, Boldon (now in Tyne and Wear) on 23 October 1934. A man called Holdcroft (who was not charged) had hired the hall from the trustees. On the night, 400 people paid 2d each to see a short of 15 minutes, followed by a longer film of $1\frac{1}{4}$ hours. They included Inspector Gargate and Sergeant Slack of the Durham Police, who took samples of the films. After forensic examination, the ten trustees were charged with allowing their premises to be used for an exhibition of inflammable films. The two men who had run the show on the night – Roland Park, a local photographer, and Ivan Seruya of Grays Inn Road, London – were charged with aiding and abetting.

When the case reached the Jarrow Police Court on 22 January 1935, Park and Seruya were defended by W. H. Thompson, a solicitor and member of the Council's executive. Funds for the defence had been raised by NCCL and the British Institute of Adult Education. The case hinged around a lengthy cross-examination of the Home Office expert, Lt. Col. Simmons, by Thompson. Were the films inflammable? The expert said that by his tests they were. The trouble was, as the clerk of the court pointed out, most things burn when subjected to sufficient heat. Lt. Col. Simmons was not prepared to say whether the films were dangerous. He professed not to know that such films were used without restriction in schools, etc. He said there were no true non-inflammable films in this country commercially.

After retiring, the magistrates dismissed the charges, and awarded costs of 25 guineas (a substantial sum in those days) to Thompson, and 7 guineas to the local solicitor who had defended the trustees. The police gave notice of appeal, but on consideration decided not to pursue the matter.

These hearings were largely technical, because the 1909 Act refers to inflammable films, not to celluloid and cellulose–acetate films. Thus, each piece of film which was the subject of a prosecution was often tested with a naked flame. Thomson, who dealt with several of these cases, derived grim pleasure from watching police witnesses desperately trying to set fire to 'non-flam' footage with a succession of matches.

In the end, the Home Office was not able to amend the legislation in such a way as to bring the 'non-flam' films under control. However, this did not stop the police from harassing 'non-flam' shows, without the slightest pretext of legality.

Writing in October 1934, Ivor Montagu referred to screenings of *Battleship Potemkin*: 'In a number of instances police authorities have advised the occupiers of the unlicensed premises about to be used that the performances are illegal. This has been an obvious excess of authority as the law now stands, and where the performances have proceeded and prosecution been invited it has in no case followed.'[28]

Only after a report, which the Home Office commissioned in 1938 (and which completed its work in the following year) recommended tactical retreat, did the authorities leave 'non-flam' films in peace. A circular was issued to local authorities finally that 'non-flam' films were outside the scope of the 1909 Act.

The censorship of the 'standard' films by the BBFC was, of course, at least as sinister as the threats to the 'non-flam' films.

During the late 1930s, the Board was hostile to any anti-Fascist or socialist work. It effectively prevented *Love on the Dole* from being filmed; it maliciously delayed certification of a peace film produced in connection with the League of Nations; it banned a pacifist film in 1935; it drastically cut *The March of Time*, 'which presented an anti-Fascist account of contemporary European history';[29] and in 1939 the anti-Nazi *Professor Mamlock* was also banned, possibly because it was Russian. By a typical historical irony, it was readily certificated once the war broke out in September.

THE HARWORTH COLLIERY AFFAIR

We have seen how the establishment's sympathy for Fascist ideology – or, at the very least, an extreme hostility to the anti-Fascists – led to gross partiality. The miners of Harworth in Nottinghamshire were also to discover that, having once taken the decision to strike and thus threaten the profits of the mine-owners, they could expect only the roughest justice. At almost all stages in this grim affair, NCCL was actively publicising and defending, pleading and denouncing. D. N. Pritt, Stafford Cripps, and, of course, Kidd himself, were all involved at crucial stages. For all their best efforts, they had little success.

The background to the dispute was as follows. There was considerable hostility between the Notts Miners' Association, and a new body called the Miners' Industrial Union (colloquially, the 'Spencer' union, after its founder) which was formed in 1926 after the General Strike. The mine managers refused to recognise more than one union and they would only deal with the MIU, which they found more cooperative. Despite the fact that a miners' ballot was held in November 1936, showing conclusively (1175 for; 145 against) that the men wished the NMA to represent their interests, the managers continued to refuse to recognise it. It was in this already tense atmosphere that a dispute arose over 'snap-time' (a refreshment break). Two men were sacked and on 2 September 1936, the miners went on strike.

The colliery called in strike-breakers, and the strikers themselves organised regular pickets in an effort to dissuade the strike-breakers from entering the colliery. All these pickets were entirely peaceful. However, reports began to reach Kidd in London that police were harassing the whole mining community whilst the strike was in progress, and he went up to Harworth early in 1937 to investigate for himself. His findings appeared in an NCCL report published in March. Here are extracts from some of the statements he took from the family of a striking miner:

Mrs S. Bircoates: 'On December 16th 1936, three police officers were found inside my house on my return from fetching Fish and Chips from a motor van which stopped at the top of the road. I had to wait some little time at the van for a second frying. During my absence, my husband, who was emptying a teapot in the outside lavatory, returned to find two police officers standing inside the passage where it leads into the sittingroom. He expressed surprise at their presence and they followed him into the sittingroom *uninvited*. Later, a third officer entered. All three officers were interviewing my husband when I returned. Next morning a large number of footprints of police boots were visible in the garden and a number of cabbage plants had been destroyed by being trampled on. On December 26th 1936, at 11.30 pm Sergeant Weaver and Inspector Eyley and a constable came to my house and told me I must not be seen on the streets when the men are coming from and going to work.'

Mr R. Bircoates: 'On January 3rd 1937, at about 10.15 pm, along with a group of other men, we were approached by Sergeant Weaver and told that we had got to stop parading the street and the best thing we could do was to clear out of the village.'

Mrs T. Bircoates: 'On December 18th 1936, Superintendent Wilson and Sergeant Weaver visited me at home at about 8.30 pm and told me that I must not be seen on the streets at the times that the men were going on or off work and that I must do my shopping outside those hours . . . I was also told that if the windows were broken at a house nearly opposite I should be held responsible and the officer added that if he caught me on the street he would "nab" me.'[30]

Thus, the police had two objectives. One was to harass and intimidate the strikers and their families; the other was to attempt to protect the strike-breakers from abuse or attack by clearing the streets during the hours when they were going to and from the colliery.

The strikers faced other hazards too, according to the NCCL report. Because the colliery village was largely owned by the mine-owners, the strikers were in constant fear of eviction. Furthermore, they were denied the use of the parish hall for any meeting connected with the strike. Kidd remarks: 'I am satisfied that the Company have used their economic power to deprive the men of their civil right of freedom of assembly.'[31]

On 23 April 1937, a month after the publication of the report, violence broke out in the village. At 9.30 pm as some strike-breakers were leaving the colliery gates, a number of stones were thrown: some at the houses of those working in the pit, some at the Miners' Institute, which had excluded the strikers since the stoppage had been declared the previous September. The Institute windows were broken. One policeman and one strike-breaker were also hit by stones, and both sustained minor cuts and bruises. Apart from this there were no injuries, and very little other damage to property. Seventeen people were arrested that evening and a day later police raided a dance hall and arrested a further five.

By the time of the police court hearing, thirty-four people were brought before the magistrates. Stafford Cripps had gone down to Nottinghamshire to defend them. Half of them were bound over, acquitted, or were given very short sentences of imprisonment. However, seventeen were sent to the Assizes for trial. It was the conduct of this trial, and the resulting sentences, which caused the greatest sense of outrage in the whole affair. In view of the minimal damage to property and the lack of serious injuries, the severity of these sentences was extraordinary: Michael Kane was sent down for two years' hard labour; Chandler and Smith got fifteen months; ten others received terms ranging from four to nine months. Perhaps even more objectionable was the nature of the evidence given at the trial by Superintendent Wilson; quite improperly he used the fact of the defendant's participation in the strike to discredit their characters. He said of one accused after another: 'During the course of the dispute he has taken an active and prominent part in hostile demonstrations against men continuing to work . . .'. Of Michael Kane, Wilson said: 'He is described as a bad workman. . . . He has been mainly responsible for the extreme bitterness which has characterised the dispute.' The lawyer who wrote the article on the case for *Civil Liberty* commented with bitter irony: 'No doubt the judge was not influenced by the irrelevant considerations put before him by the police superintendent. No doubt the sentence he gave would have been exactly the same whether or not Superintendent Wilson had described Michael Kane as a good or a bad workman.'[32]

After the trial, NCCL got up a petition to the Home Secretary asking for the remission of the harsh sentences. When presented on 8 September, it had a quarter of a million signatures. On a second front, Pritt appeared in the Court of Criminal Appeal on an application for leave to appeal; this was denied. Eventually, after continuing public pressure, the Home Secretary did grant some remission of the sentences.

Something Kidd said in his report, before the disturbances occurred, appears in retrospect peculiarly appropriate: 'In an industrial dispute of this nature it is most unfortunate that the Bench before which offences arising out of the strike are tried, is composed almost exclusively of persons whose social and economic background is that of the Mineowners rather than of the men. Respect for law is gravely prejudiced by a widespread belief (whether justified or otherwise) that consciously or unconsciously the local Magistrates favour the owners rather than the miners.'[33]

THE 'SEDITION' BILL

In 1931, there was a mutiny among the fleet at Invergordon. As a result, it was felt that there was an urgent need to strengthen the law against sedition and in 1934 the Incitement to Disaffection Bill was introduced in the House of Commons. NCCL's opposition to the Bill was well supported by other groups, and although the legislation eventually went through, improvements were effected because of the campaign.

The Bill, intended to replace the Mutiny Act of 1797, made it an offence to seduce a member of His Majesty's forces from his duty or allegiance. From the first, this innocent word 'or' was at the centre of protest, for the 1797 Act had spoken of 'duty *and* allegiance'. It was going to be much easier to get convictions under the new Bill. Despite its best efforts, the Council was unable to change the 'or' back into an 'and' before the Bill passed into law.

There were, however, four changes which were conceded under pressure. The initial draft had omitted the words 'maliciously and advisedly', which were to be found in the Incitement to Mutiny Act, and which in that Act restricted the liability of potential defendants. The phrase was re-inserted, although it proved to be rather feeble protection, as Kidd pointed out in 1940: 'Mr Justice Humphreys has ruled that "maliciously" only means "deliberately", and as all actions in our waking moments are deliberate, this amendment did nothing to alter the meaning of the clause.'[34] More importantly, the Bill at first made it an offence to possess documents which could be used seditiously, whether or not their owner had any such intention; the onus was placed on the defendant to justify his/her ownership. This was redrafted to include the phrase, 'with intent to commit or to aid, abet, counsel, or procure the commission of an offence' and the onus of proof thus shifted over to the prosecution again. A third change concerned the search powers in the Bill. In the final version, it would have to be a High Court judge, rather than a magistrate, who could authorise a search warrant. Fourthly, the Bill had originally proposed to make it illegal to do 'an act preparatory' to the substantive offence. This was going much further than the ordinary rules about *attempting* crimes. Professor Harry Street explains:

> . . . English law recognises as a matter of course that one who does not actually commit a crime may nonetheless be convicted of an *attempt* where he has done an act with intent to commit that offence, and where that act is a step towards the commission of that offence which is immediately connected with it. If, therefore, the Bill had been silent about attempts, they would still have constituted crimes as long as they fell within the definition in the previous sentence. But the Bill did not stop there.[35]

No indeed. Street amusingly suggests that even to board a train for Portsmouth might fall within the meaning of preparatory acts. Street could have gone on to point out that the substantive offence is not *actually* seducing soldiers and sailors, but *endeavouring* to do so. Had the 'preparatory act' clause been retained (it was not), it would have been possible for a defendant to be charged with performing an act preparatory to attempting to endeavour to seduce from their duty or allegiance members of the forces!

The Council's campaign against the Bill established the importance of forming alliances across party lines. One of the most eminent lawyers to speak out against the proposed measures, Sir William Holdsworth, KC, Vinerian Professor of

Law in the University of Oxford, was a Conservative. He referred to the Bill as 'the most daring encroachment upon the liberty of the subject which the Executive Government has yet attempted at a time which is not a time of emergency.'[36] The *Law Journal* wrote an editorial attacking the Bill; seventeen lawyers issued a manifesto on the same lines. Even the *Army, Navy and Air Force Gazette* came out against it. Within forty-eight hours of the publication of the Bill, NCCL had sent briefings about its dangers to every MP. Two weeks later, it had organised a meeting at the Conway Hall, and this was followed by another at the Kingsway Hall chaired by the Dean of Canterbury. This in turn led to a delegate conference at the Memorial Hall, with 1600 representatives. Support came from all quarters: the National Peace Council, the National Liberal Federation, the London Trades Council, and a host of political, academic, legal, industrial, religious and pacifist groups. Two mass rallies (in June and October) were held in Trafalgar Square. The Council's annual report for 1934 emphasised the breadth of support, from all sections of the community, evident at the October meeting: 'Here every diverse element was fused – Socialist and individualist, Conservative and Liberal, Quaker and Communist – united by a determination to voice in no uncertain terms their abhorrence of this attempt to reverse fundamental principles of British law.' The extent of the dismay amongst informed sections of the public, and the resulting combined assault, reminds one of nothing so much as the campaign against the notorious Police and Criminal Evidence Bill of 1982, which, at the time of writing (December 1983) is once again before Parliament.

The campaign was not all heavy-hearted drudgery; members obviously enjoyed themselves at the Friends' House, Euston Road, on 6 November:

The trial made excellent propaganda by exposing to ridicule and laughter the follies of this dangerous measure. An enthusiastic audience filled the hall to overflowing, and crowds had to be turned away. 'Low' was in the dock,

accused of seducing from his allegiance – by means of his
famous 'Sedition' Bill cartoon – a soldier, played with
delightful drollery by Mr Kingsley Martin. Mr Low, as the
star performer, delighted the big audience with his comedy
and with his lightning caricature of the learned and senile
Judge (amusingly impersonated by Mr Aylmer Vallance,
Editor of the 'News Chronicle'). Mr Miles Malleson con-
vulsed his audience by his comedy policeman. The absurdities of the Bill were tellingly underlined by Mr Graham
Hutton (counsel for the prosecution) and by W. H. Thomson
(counsel for the defence). The comedy of the evening was
rounded off by the personal appearance in the witness-box of
our old friend 'Colonel Blimp' of the 'Evening Standard'. At
the end of the trial Mr Aylmer Vallance auctioned the
caricature of himself for eight guineas.[37]

After all the commotion over the Act, it is ironic that only one
prosecution took place before the Act was revived in 1972. This
first prosecution was brought against an eighteen-year-old
student from Leeds called Ronald Phillips. Phillips had what
sounds like a most bizarre conversation in a café with Corporal
Crabtree, who seems to have pretended to have been disaf-
fected with the RAF. His interlocutor was thus encouraged to
suggest various fantastic schemes: the theft of a plane with
which to fly to Spain to fight against Franco, and the idea that
Crabtree ought to try to convert his entire squadron to
revolutionary fervour. Crabtree, armed to the teeth with these
incriminating remarks, turned him in. Phillips was sent to
prison for twelve months. Vyvyan Adams, a Conservative MP
who supported civil liberties' issues, helped to get this harsh
sentence reduced to a few months, by appealing to the Home
Secretary. The awful majesty of the law had yet again shown its
mettle; the public had been saved from the danger of a very silly
teenager (Kidd calls him 'an irresponsible lad'[38]) having an
even sillier conversation with a man whose subsequent conduct
in betraying Phillips showed that nobody and nothing could
seduce *him*.

In 1937, on his way to address a meeting in Hampstead, Kidd was knocked over by a car. He suffered a broken leg, and was rushed to hospital. 'The shock of the impact when the car ran into him half way over the Belisha crossing must have told on his system – and his heart', recalls Sylvia Scaffardi. 'Discharged, he was glad to resume normal work. But he was lugging a leg encased in heavy plaster from ankle to thigh.'[39] As the war began, he became increasingly ill. 'By 1941 his heart was at times behaving quite erratically but he was never absent sick from NCCL, till the end. Up till then he was always prepared to work on indefinitely.'[40]

Differences arose within the executive committee of the Council, some of whom obviously thought that Kidd was 'past his best'. The man who had founded the organisation and who was totally committed to the civil liberty cause found himself under pressure to drop some of the more arduous work. It was finally agreed that he become 'Director' of the Council and that a new general secretary be appointed.

The person being groomed for the job was Elizabeth Allen, who had come onto the staff in 1941 as Appeals Officer after some years as Joint Secretary of the International Peace Campaign, based in Geneva. Kidd, desperately ill, was grieved to find himself unable even to take up the limited duties of Director. Clearly dying, he was forced to stand down and Elizabeth Allen took his place.

He died in May 1942. There were death notices in the national and provincial press. The BBC carried obituaries, including one on its Empire Service by Kingsley Martin. Telegrams and messages flooded into the office, from as far afield as Africa and the West Indies.

At the funeral, E. M. Forster paid him tribute, referring to 'his stubborn courage, his loyalty, his refusal to admit defeat, his adherence to principles'. He also said of him: 'He knew that freedom is not the perquisite of any one section of the community: neither the employing classes nor the artistic and literary classes can be truly free unless all are free.'[41]

But the final word should rest with Sylvia Scaffardi, Kidd's companion in the formative years of NCCL: 'Ronald himself never thought about his single-minded commitment to NCCL as self-sacrifice, it was for him a labour of love, what he wanted to do. The passionate Irishman in him made him happy to devote himself to accuracy, taking up time to dot the i's and cross the t's. NCCL soon had a reputation with news editors for reliability.'

'But the best memorial Ronald Kidd was to have was the perpetuation of NCCL and its effectiveness today. Its survival (when so many progressive bodies of the 30s served their term and expired) was due not only to the urgent need for such a body but also because it was established on sound lines.'[42]

2 1939–45

Britain declared war on Germany on 3 September 1939. Even before this, however, in August, Parliament had passed the Emergency Powers Act, under which the government was able to introduce a whole series of Defence Regulations (DRs). Because they affected all the areas which NCCL dealt with, it is hardly surprising that most of the Council's efforts during the six years of war were directed at attempting to mitigate the injustices frequently caused by these regulations. Very often, however, the authorities stayed with the more 'traditional' methods of harassing their opponents, such as the use of 'obstruction' or 'insulting behaviour' charges.

DISSENT

On 21 October 1939, two men who were handing out pacifist leaflets at Willesden Labour Exchange were arrested. It might have been possible for the police to secure a conviction against the men under DR 39, which made it an offence to attempt to influence public opinion 'in a manner likely to be prejudicial to the defence of the realm, or to the efficient prosecution of the war'. Instead, the perennial charge of 'obstructing the footpath' was trundled out. As it happened, the prosecution was unsuccessful, but the police had managed to keep the pacifists away from the Exchange (where people registered for military service) for a full six hours. Similarly, an anti-war speaker at Worthing who held up to his audience pictures of mutilated faces from a book, found himself charged with being a rogue and a vagabond under Section 4 of the Vagrancy Act of 1934, for showing obscene pictures in a public place. Distributors of Communist Party leaflets often found themselves victimised. In June 1940, three people were giving out leaflets which included the words: 'Britain needs a Government based of working people, a Government in which there is no friend of Fascism.'[1] The charge was 'using insulting words and behaviour' and they were each fined £50 and sent to prison for three months, with hard labour.

Many of these incidents, which involved quite blatant attempts by the authorities to stifle dissent, were taken up by the Council. For example, a student at Twickenham Art School was found with a copy of the *Daily Worker* and a pamphlet called *War and the Workers*. The headmaster promptly called the police, who not only questioned the boy but told him at the end of the interrogation not to mention it to anyone! NCCL protested about this incident to the Middlesex County Council; but in other more serious cases the Council provided full legal services. At the Stratford Police Court, for instance, four people were charged with insulting behaviour whilst distributing political material outside a factory. They spent a week in the cells – as usual in these cases, bail was refused – and were then sentenced to three months' imprisonment. NCCL sponsored an appeal, which was successful in having the sentence commuted to a binding over.

It was especially discouraging that the mania for enforcing conformity was by no means restricted to the police and the judiciary. The academic world afforded many depressing cases of intolerance. Two student members of the University of Exeter Socialist Society were sent down in May 1940. One of them, Mr Lee, had written a letter to the college newspaper, *The South-Westerner*, which ended with the following passage: 'The star of hope, rising above the Volga and the Hoang-Ho, shines with a dimmed but steady lustre through the foul smoke and stench of the European scene. Today is the testing time of men.'[2] Whilst the literary bombast might be exceptionable (one likes to think Mr Lee was not reading for an English degree) the Principal's view that the sentiments were highly subversive is mere silliness. The supposed offence of the other undergraduate was equally footling; he had spoken against the setting up of a National Savings Group in the students' Guild Council. At the same time as the sending down of the two students, the University ruled that all meetings of student societies, and all distribution of periodicals, was forthwith banned unless permission was obtained from the deans.

At Loughborough College, conscientious objectors seeking jobs were refused testimonials and references, on the grounds that they should not be in a position to start their careers earlier than those who had enlisted. At Bangor, postgraduate studentships were abandoned because only conscientious objectors would benefit. Liverpool students broke up a Peace Pledge Union meeting, and at Oxford, students attacked a May Day procession. A proctor at Cambridge wrote to the Union Society suggesting that it would be in 'good taste' if debates were discontinued for the duration of the war. The dogged persistence of the anti-libertarians is well illustrated in the case of Dr Peate. He was Keeper of the Department of Folk Culture at the National Museum of Wales and internationally acclaimed as a leading authority in his field. The Ministry of Labour had agreed to accord Dr Peate's job the status of a reserved occupation. The museum authorities, incensed at what they took to be Peate's lack of patriotism, and further galled because he was known as a pacifist, pressed the Ministry of Labour to change its mind and to de-reserve the entire museum staff. In this they were successful. To avoid conscription, Peate was now forced to register as a conscientious objector, which he did in July 1941. In August, the council of the museum dismissed Peate, and it was at this point that the South Wales branch of NCCL began campaigning on his behalf. They held meetings and wrote to the papers, so that by the time the museum met in October to decide whether or not to ratify the dismissal, Peate's case had become something of a *cause célèbre*. All the Welsh MPs were members of the Court of

Governors and amongst those giving Peate support was Lloyd George, now almost eighty. Although the governors decided that Peate should be re-instated (the vote was 38 to 19) the museum's council still were not giving in. They demoted Peate to Assistant Keeper, at the same time saying that they might consider re-instating him to his former position if he satisfactorily completed a 'probationary period'.

It was clear that in this climate of bigotry, celebrity was no shield. This had been made clear to Peate, and it was also made apparent to Mr Nicholas of Aberystwyth. Nicholas was a very highly regarded Welsh poet, but it was his membership of the Communist Party which got him into trouble. He was arrested in July 1940, and the account of his interrogation in the dead of night, by the Chief Constable, makes extraordinary reading. When Nicholas was ushered into his presence, the Chief Constable immediately shouted at him: 'Sit down, I have got you at last. I have been waiting for this chance'.[3] A dentist friend called Williams also had a hard time in the interviewing room. The exchange, as described in *Civil Liberty No 20*, has all the expected narrow-mindedness. But I wonder if I am being fanciful in detecting, between the lines, a subtle triumphant contempt which Williams is directing at his interrogator:

> The Chief Constable questioned him about the leaflet which he was alleged to have distributed and suggested that Mr Williams had become a Socialist through the influence of Mr Nicholas. To which Mr Williams replied that he had become a Socialist through the late Keir Hardie and the late Mr Ramsey Macdonald, both personal friends of his. The Chief Constable then questioned him as to literature which he suggested Mr Williams had obtained from Russia. To which Mr Williams replied that he had in fact bought it from Messrs W H Smith's.[4]

There was great local indignation at the arrest of Mr Nicholas and his son (who had been taken into custody at the same time as his father). At an NCCL conference held on 24

August 1940, a resolution was passed demanding the trial or release of the pair; four weeks later they were freed after an advisory committee recommended this step to the Home Secretary. The son wrote shortly afterwards to the Council: 'We fully appreciate that were it not for your practical interest and active intervention we would not have reached this happy conclusion . . .'.[5]

The Nicholases were held in detention under the notorious regulation 18B, which, of all the Defence Regulations, was the most bitterly resented. It provided that the Secretary of State could authorise the detention of anyone at any time; as there was no appeal to the courts (though the accused could lodge an objection to an advisory committee) the measure effectively suspended *habeas corpus*. The feeling against 18B was so strong (and NCCL shares the credit for agitating against it) that by the end of 1939 it was slightly watered down. Under the new dispensation, the Secretary of State could only authorise a detention order if he had reasonable cause to suspect the person of 'hostile origin or association' or of having been recently concerned in acts prejudicial to the defence of the realm. In the Nicholas case, the advisory committee recommended release, and this was done.

Those who fell foul of the Defence Regulations seem almost always to have been on the political left; members of the Left Book Club were particularly vulnerable. DR 88A provided very wide powers of search, and police were constantly hauling off supposedly subversive works. John Stuart Mill's *Principles of Political Economy* and Ernest Hemingway's *Farewell to Arms* were amongst the impoundees.

Local Communist Parties were constantly being harassed. In South Wales, a Communist Party branch informed the Chief Constable that it intended to hold an open-air meeting; the Chief Constable tried to pretend that no such meeting could be held unless he issued a permit, which he declined to do. NCCL was able to point out to the meeting's organisers that the Defence Regulations did not contain any mention of permits for meetings, and in the event the meeting was duly held, unmolested, with NCCL observers in attendance. In Gravesend, the Communist Party branch had great difficulty getting a poster advertising a meeting printed; a bill-posting company also gave trouble, insisting that police permission would be needed before they could accept the job. A local newspaper in the town declined to accept an advertisement for the meeting. NCCL suspected that the Gravesend police had brought pressure to bear on these various commercial concerns.

The level of public hysteria and petty suspicion comes across with particular force in the case of Mrs Ryecraft. She had founded, and become president of, the Wood Green Housewives' Club. Many witnesses spoke of the value of the Club's discussions to its members: 'My happiest afternoons were at the meetings', 'the meetings were most cheerful', 'I could not wish for anything different', 'I went to the Club for a good afternoon. I think the discussions are a good thing and very helpful'.[6] She was charged under DR 39B, the famous 'alarm and despondency' regulation, for making gloomy remarks about the food situation and also for saying that the only way to end the war was for British and German workers to unite. Although she was readily acquitted, the chairman of the court made it clear that, had it been proved that the defendant had suggested that Britain might not win the war, and had her hearers taken her view as authoritative, then she would have truly found herself in trouble.

Of course, one of the commonest forms of dissent during the war was conscientious objection. Whilst being prepared to join the fight assiduously for the rights of conscientious objectors, NCCL remained neutral on the issue itself. An article which appeared in *Civil Liberty* late in 1939 made this clear: 'It is no part of the function of the National Council for Civil Liberties to lay down a principle as to whether people should or should not participate in armed service.'[7]

Tribunals were set up to determine whether those wishing to register as conscientious objectors were sincere and genuine. A constant difficulty stemmed from the fact that the meaning of 'conscientious' was not defined in the National Service Act 1939, whose provisions governed the administration of military conscription. In the November 1939 issue of *Civil Liberty*, NCCL complained that the tribunals regularly construed the term 'conscientious' only in a religious sense, so that those who had a moral abhorrence of killing based on rationalism often found themselves discriminated against. The experience of George Plume illustrates some of the difficulties. He had successfully registered as a conscientious objector on political grounds, and as a result the Minister of Labour appealed against the decision. The Ministry of Labour officials conceded that 'There is nothing in the Act which limits conscientious objectors to objections which are based solely on religious grounds.'[8] Nevertheless, they then went on to distinguish between political objectors and other non-religious ones, using the argument that political objectors only had a *conditional* objection whilst some humanists, for example, could be said to object *absolutely*. NCCL consistently argued that both forms of objection were equally valid.

Much more extraordinary was the statement of the Chairman, when Plume's case came up before the Appeal Tribunal. He took it upon himself, before any witnesses or evidence had been heard, to divine the real meaning behind the perplexing terminology:

> The intention of the Statute was not to protect every form of conscientious objection; it was not intended to protect the Fascist who has an objection to fighting for the Government . . . it was not intended to protect a Socialist who may have a conscientious objection to fighting for a Capitalist State. . . . You are on much safer ground if you can plead as a pacifist than if you plead any particular programme, because it is submitted that they are excluded under the terms of the Act.[9]

Plume lost the case. The Appeal Tribunal, seeming almost to apologise for its quirky logic, gave its decision 'without making any final precedent'.[10] But it was taken as a precedent. On 9

November, R. W. Sorensen asked the Minister of Labour, in the Commons, whether political grounds for objection were or were not valid for the purposes of the tribunals. 'That is still the idea', the minister replied, in a marvellously slippery phrase that manages to combine an intellectual commitment to the proposition, with an implied view that anyone who relied on it would be chancing their luck.

Outside the tribunals, the Council was concerned with the victimisation of those who had already successfully registered as conscientious objectors. Local authorities were especially bad at this. In South Wales, one corporation demanded that all its employees sign a 'declaration of loyalty' to 'the aims of the State'. As the declaration contained a commitment to be 'whole heartedly in support of the ruthless prosecution of the war'[11] one of the teachers in an Elementary School, who was a conscientious objector, refused to sign and he was dismissed. He managed to get himself re-instated, however, by digging out Circular 1522 (which concerned employment protection) and successfully flourishing it in the faces of his adversaries. Elsewhere, in Altrincham, Colchester and Northwich, conscientious objectors were either sacked or harassed. Usually, this was just for the duration of the war, but the London County Council dismissed a local government officer outright, once he had registered.

Private employers could be just as bad. A man working in the office of a colliery in the Midlands was told by his bosses that his colleagues were not prepared to work with him (although this was not true) and that therefore he had to be sacked. Another man was dismissed from the Royal Schools of Music in London, on the pretext that no conscientious objector could be employed in any establishment under royal patronage.

It is sad to find that conscientious objectors often found their own fellow workers hostile. In Hinckley, factory workers actually went on strike to force the suspension of a conscientious objector, and there was a similar case in Newmarket. 'These intolerant workers', sighed the writer in *Civil Liberty*, 'should at any rate have a higher level of political education than the militaristic Town Councillors and reactionary employers.'[12]

THE EMPIRE

NCCL now concerns itself only with events in England, Wales and Northern Ireland. Even Scotland has, since 1974, been excluded from its remit, as the concern of a sister body, the Scottish Council for Civil Liberties. Yet in the early years, Britain's continuing role as a colonial power encouraged the Council to take an extensive interest in the affairs of the colonies, and, indeed, of the world at large.

The 1934 Annual Report gives an account of a delegation from the Gold Coast (now Ghana) which had come to London to protest at the Colonial Office about various abuses. When the Colonial Secretary refused to receive it, NCCL organised a meeting in the House of Commons between some Liberal MPs and the delegation. The Council was also able to help them get some good press coverage.

Labour conditions in Kenya also constituted an issue in which the Council showed great interest. In 1939 it organised a weekend conference on the subject, at which Archdeacon W. E. Owen, with thirty five years' experience of East Africa, gave a full account of the injustices suffered by the people. He revealed the details of the penal sanctions associated with employment contracts. In the first place, 'recruitment' of labour was little short of press-ganging; once individuals became, in law, 'employees', they were subject to monstrous conditions of service. Absenteeism, careless work and disobedience were all offences punishable by one month's imprisonment. There was a penalty of £150 for 'harbouring a runaway labourer'. Fourteen thousand children (minimum age for work, ten) were employed in the colony, half of them in the tea industry. The nature of their work frequently meant that they were separated more or less permanently from their parents.

It was the disturbances in Trinidad in June of 1937 which became the focus for NCCL's chief campaign on colonial issues in the pre-war period. There had been serious disorder on the island, largely as a result of extreme poverty, poor health and bad housing. The British Government responded by establishing a commission of inquiry. When this commission produced a report, it was the subject of a special meeting organised by NCCL, which was held in the Conway Hall on 4 March 1938. Arthur Creech Jones, MP, who had in fact written for *Civil Liberty*, was one of the speakers. So too was Harold Moody, president of the League of Coloured Peoples. By the time war broke out the following year, the Council had a good deal of colonial work under its belt.

Some of the repressive measures being taken abroad purported to constitute a necessary revision of legislation. In Sierra Leone, for example, the 'ordinances' introduced by the colonial government, at the instigation of the Secretary of State for the Colonies, included provisions for the deportation of certain residents (those domiciled for less than seven years) if they were, for example, destitute or 'undesirable'. The definition of an 'undesirable' person was one 'who is or has been conducting himself so as to be dangerous to peace, good order, good government or public morals'.[13] Not only was this deportation ordinance unacceptably broad in its definitions, but the judge whose decision it would be as to whether a person was to be deported was not bound by the ordinary rules affecting the admissibility of evidence. NCCL played a major part in lobbying against the ordinance, and had the minor satisfaction of prevailing upon Malcolm MacDonald, the Colonial Secretary, to alter the provisions so that at least some regard would be paid by the judge to the usual rules of evidence. More gratifying, NCCL helped to get deleted the entire section of the ordinance which provided that 'no writ of Habeas Corpus or other process calling in question the legality of any order made under this Ordinance shall have any effect'.[14] Had this provision not been left out, all kinds of abuses in the administration of justice – most obviously, detention without legal safeguards – would have been the certain result.

A separate ordinance, dealing with sedition, made it an offence merely to possess seditious literature; this was based, of course, on the same clause which had appeared in Britain's own Incitement of Disaffection Act 1934, but which had been thrown out as a result of considerable pressure. No luck there, but the council managed to help effect a small change in regard to the undesirable literature ordinance. As originally drafted, the importation of anything 'contrary to the public interest' could be banned. NCCL felt that some improvement had occurred when this was made specific and a list was drawn up to embrace publications deemed 'indecent, obscene, seditious, defamatory, blasphemous, scandalous or demoralising'.[15] For my part, this seems considerably worse than the original formula, insofar as it is almost impossible to imagine what categories of books likely to incur official disapproval could possibly escape prosecution under the new dispensation.

Where colonial matters were in question, the Council often made representations to MacDonald in conjunction with the League of Coloured Peoples. This was the case in 1939 when the Colonial Secretary received a delegation from both bodies in connection with the allegations of torture, by rubbing pepper into sensitive parts of the body, in Sierra Leone, in order to extract the payment of taxes. MacDonald's answer to the complainants is outrageous; virtually accepting that the torture had in fact taken place with the connivance of government officials, he did no more than advance the usual formula that 'it was open to the victims to take civil action against their tormentors if they wished to do so'.[16] The expense, delays and intimidating nature of such a course of litigation effectively left most victims without a remedy.

In February 1941, NCCL organised a conference on colonial affairs which was held in London, and was attended by delegates from 235 organisations. An especially valuable feature of the event was the pooling of information and experience; the conference afforded 'excellent memoranda on conditions in the various Colonies which were circulated to the delegates'.[17] In November of the same year, the NCCL executive responded to the arrest of Pandit Nehru by passing a resolution urging the government to release him and his political colleagues.

Commercial exploitation was also taken up by NCCL. In its pamphlet, *Civil Liberty and the Colonies*, produced by the Overseas Sub-Committee, the Council listed some of the persistent malpractices. For example, in the Gold Coast, local coffee growers had to sell their crops to the European monopoly concerns, which fixed the prices without consultation. In Trinidad, a trade union newspaper calld *Vanguard* attacked the administration for the manner in which the sugar subsidy was paid out in 1944. The large business corporations received 60 per cent of the money, the remaining 40 per cent having to be shared out amongst 14 000 small farmers.

In the career structure of the colonial administrations, Europeans had a virtual monopoly of the most prestigious jobs. When there was a vacancy in Lagos for Town Clerk, NCCL aptly summed up the situation: 'It was not, of course, suggested that Africans as such were debarred from the job; it was only suggested that none were so suitable as the rival European applicant.'[18] It was equally invidious that pay scales were based on race; throughout Nigeria, an African magistrate was paid £200 less than a European one. The Council's view of this job inequality pointed out the contradiction of the whole colonial enterprise. On the one hand, Britain was governing other nations on the pretext that the colonial process was one of gradually acclimatising local populations to Western concepts of good order and government, and on the other hand she was withholding precisely those opportunities for experiencing power without which the whole venture, even on its own terms, was meaningless.

Needless to say, educational provision reflected this hypocrisy; for whereas it was persistently argued that the various territories could not be placed in the hands of the majority of

their inhabitants until the standard of education made democratic majority rule practicable, it was also the case that
moneys spent on that educational provision were so parsimoni-
ous as almost to postpone forever the attainment of the
supposedly indispensable standard.

It was, perhaps, the administration of taxes which caused the
greatest resentment. The worst culprit was the Poll Tax, levied
on a *per capita* basis, and bearing no relation to individual
incomes. The effect of it – indeed, its very *raison d'être* – was to
force workers to leave the land and find work on the planta-
tions, or in the mines, where they would earn enough to pay the
tax. It was, in other words, a crudely disguised form of
semi-slavery which also separated families: husbands from
wives, sons from their parents. The figures given by Lord
Hailey in his *African Survey* of the number of 'able-bodied males'
permanently absent from home are appalling: 17 per cent in
Nyasaland (now Malawi), 33 per cent in parts of Rhodesia
(now Zimbabwe), 40 per cent in Swaziland and fully 50 per
cent in Basutoland. Of course, the Poll Tax was always fixed so
that it would take a sufficient proportion of a labourer's wages
to ensure that the labourer could not save any money after
paying living expenses, and would have to continue working
year after year. And although in cash terms Europeans in the
colonies paid higher taxes as individuals, their contributions as
a proportion of income were far lower than those of the
indigenous population. The latter's tax liability represented
between 30–50 per cent of earnings, whereas the European
figure rarely exceeded 10 per cent.

Throughout this period the hated 'pass laws', which today
we associate with South Africa, obtained in the whole of British
colonial Africa. In East Africa, it was forbidden to leave a
reserve without a special pass; those wishing to go out after
9 pm also needed a special night pass; passes had to be carried
as proof that Poll Tax payments were up to date; in Kenya,
workers had to carry records signed by employers, and
containing finger prints; in Rhodesia, railway tickets were only
sold to those who could produce employers' permits at the

booking office. The entire Pass Law system was based on two premises: first, that those who worked for the commercial enterprises could not only be treated badly in their general conditions of employment, but could be refused the most basic civil liberties such as freedom of movement; secondly, and equally squalid in moral terms, the law was being used as a vehicle for the employers' financial interests, without the slightest pretext of any jurisprudential fairness.

The harshness of these laws was not mitigated by any slackness in their enforcement. In 1935, there were 20 000 cases in Rhodesia alone. In South Africa, a judge called Krause reckoned that 90 per cent of the prison population had been convicted either for defaulting on payment of Poll Tax, or for a Pass Law infringement. He went on: 'A native will be lucky if within twenty-four hours of entering an urban area he does not find himself in prison.'[19]

The legal relationship between employer and worker did not simply depend on the contract between these two parties. Almost all the African colonies also had a 'Masters and Servants Act' which provided that fines, and sometimes imprisonment for up to six months, could be imposed for such offences as drunkenness, neglect of duty, absence from work without permission, refusing to carry out instructions, and insulting the employer, his wife or his daughter (though not apparently, his son!) Trades Unions were technically legal in the colonies from 1938 onwards, but in practice their power was extremely limited. For example, although forty-two colonies had Minimum Wage Laws, in only nine were they put into effect, and the unions had insufficient influence to rectify the situation.

Interference in union affairs during the war years was constant. In Nigeria in 1944, the president of the Railway Workers' Union was detained. When the paper, *Nigerian Worker*, protested about the detention, its office was raided by police and it was served with a notice under the Nigerian Defence Regulations, which meant that it had to submit all copy for pre-censorship. In Northern Rhodesia, the general secretary of the Mineworkers' Union was deported after his union had started to ask awkward questions about the drop in production. In 1940, the European mineworkers went on strike for better pay and were successful; when the African workers decided to follow suit, their strike was met with tear gas and bullets and seventeen people were killed.

In Kenya, people had been dispossessed of their land by the European settlers. They had then been labelled 'squatters' and forced to work for 180 days each year on the landowner's schemes; sometimes they were not even paid a wage, but merely fed. Those forced labour conditions also existed in various forms in the Gold Coast, Nigeria, Nyasaland, Tanganyika (now part of Tanzania), Uganda and Sierra Leone.

In October 1945, NCCL took advantage of the presence in London of colonial delegates to the World Trade Union Conference to organise a conference of its own on colonial affairs. It addressed itself in particular to the problem of how to bring to the attention of the British public the manifold abuses of civil liberties.

The muzzling of the press in the colonial territories was ruthless. The use of the defence regulations was not dissimilar to that at home, but there were also novel features. In Nigeria and the Gambia, for example, newspapers were required to place cash deposits with the authorities, and these were confiscated if the papers published anything deemed offensive.

ALIENS

At the outbreak of war, the government had to decide what to do about more than 73 000 foreigners, who were nationals of enemy countries, and who were at that time on British soil. It was decided to set up tribunals, which would divide the so-called 'enemy aliens' into three categories: those about whom grave doubts existed (Class A); those whom the tribunals considered trustworthy (Class C); and those fitting neither category (Class B). In practice, the tribunals varied enormously in the criteria they adopted; some were more reluctant to accord Class C status than others, for example. Nevertheless, most enemy aliens (64 000) were fortunate enough to find themselves in the C category and relatively few, as a percentage, found themselves in Class A (600).

Unfortunately, this tripartite system very quickly became irrelevant once the Home Office began, in the middle of 1940, to round up and intern all enemy aliens. The policy change was partly the result of greater alarm about the way the war was going, but it was also partly because Lord Rothermere's *Daily Mail*, and other sections of the press, were stirring up anti-refugee sentiment by talking about 'fifth-columnists' and the like.

A crucial legal problem now arose. Were the internments which had been carried out based on powers contained in DR 18B, or were they based on common law? The distinction was important because decisions under Defence Regulations could be challenged before advisory committees; specifically, orders under 18B from the Secretary of State had to show 'reasonable cause' for detention; and those who fell foul of the Defence Regulations were entitled to be told of the charges against them. Were it to be the case that enemy aliens were being interned under common law, none of the above three features would apply. But these common law powers can only be used once there is a state of war. The government itself was in some confusion over the issue. On 31 October 1940, the Home Secretary assured the Commons that 'where an enemy alien is concerned . . . no regulation need be invoked at all'.[20] Notwithstanding this, at the end of the same debate, the Lord Privy Seal, Sir Samuel Hoare, dismissed the suggestion that the particular Defence Regulation should be withdrawn by saying, among other things: 'The effect of this would be to leave a vacuum, and the result would be, to take a single instance, that the enemy aliens who at the moment are interned under these regulations would have to be released tomorrow morning.'[21]

The contradiction in the two statements led Kenelm Digby to quip: 'That is presumably an illustration of the constitutional doctrine of joint ministerial responsibility.'[22]

In view of the confusion, NCCL asked Dingle Foot MP to ask the Home Secretary a question on the matter in the House. Answering it, on 23 November, Sir John Anderson stated categorically that the aliens were being interned under common law powers. NCCL then drew attention to the fact that those who had been interned between the introduction of Defence Regulations in August 1939, and the declaration of war a month later, had thus been illegally detained.

The Council could not do anything about these common law detentions, but it did campaign against the actual physical conditions in the internment camps. One such camp is described thus: 'Two thousand people were housed in the main building . . . it was surrounded by two rows of barbed wire, between which armed guards patrolled . . . the floor was slippery through oil and grease. There were neither tables nor benches. We had to eat standing. The lighting of the place was through the glass roof, but as it was partly broken the rain came in also. There were eighteen water taps for 2000 people.'[23]

Newspapers and other printed information was banned for internees, and this led to great anxiety, both about global and personal matters. Ignorance bred rumours and scare stories of food shortages and imminent invasion. Incredible carelessness was demonstrated by the camps' organisers in handling the personal documents of internees, with the result that many were lost; this too caused great distress. Food was very poor and monotonous, and this lack of wholesome nutrition went hand in hand with the lack of proper medical care. Those with tuberculosis, diabetes and heart trouble frequently received no care at all. Not only were letters censored, but the delays before they were sent on their way were severe – sometimes up to four weeks. When inmates were transferred to hospital, there were no facilities for their letters to be censored and so they were not allowed to send any; the relatives of the sick could, thus, have no idea of the health of a member of their family at the critical moment. One of the most grievous sufferings that internees faced was the separation of families; many of them were sent overseas to camps in Canada and Australia, and in this way wives were separated from husbands, children from parents. The physical conditions in the Canadian camps were usually better than those in Britain, but censorship restrictions were tighter, as was access to books and journals. Additionally, special Jewish camps were set up (presumably justified on the grounds of protecting internees from the bigotry of other inmates) and many complaints were received about the anti-Semitism of those in charge of them. The Australian camps attracted fewer protests, although internees on their way to Australia on board the *Dunera* were very badly treated, many of them having their possessions confiscated or thrown over-board.

On the Isle of Man, there was a women's camp where Nazis and refugees were expected to live together amicably, and to cooperate with each other. A similar situation existed on the mainland, at Huyton, where a camp primarily designed for Nazi detainees also had an admixture of their opponents. According to Margery Corbett Ashby, then a member of NCCL's executive, the Nazi majority made life very unpleasant for the minority: '[Huyton] has been reserved for Nazis, but specially selected people – well-known leaders elected by their fellow trade unionists – have been taken from other camps . . . and have been placed with the Nazis in this camp. The Nazis control it completely and have taken over the canteen and other camp facilities. The plight of this tiny minority of known anti-Nazis among them is a desperate one'.[24]

Very many of those interned could not possibly have constituted a threat to the national interest or to security. Very many, indeed, were active anti-Fascists. A second group which was equally innocuous but also found itself confined was the section of the community, mostly from London's East End, who were of 'enemy origin'. They included two men who had been born in Poland but who had lived in England for 44 and 35 years respectively; despite the fact that their sons were registered for military service, they were still interned.

At an NCCL conference held on 21 July 1940, which had been convened to discuss the threat of the new powers of the wartime government, the Council's president, Henry Nevinson (E. M. Forster had stepped down) denounced the policy of interning aliens: 'To me, it is shameful and humiliating to see many of my friends . . . suddenly bustled off without possibility of appeal to some concentration camp, shut up under barbed wire, and deprived of communication with their friends or their wives or their children . . . I want to tell the people who are responsible for this atrocious cruelty that we know them for what they are.'[25]

The public disquiet about the conditions of internment camps and the indiscriminate way in which aliens were sent to them, led to the government agreeing to implement guidelines for the release of certain detainees. A White Paper of July 1940 lists the categories of those to be released: 'Persons under 16 or over 65, young persons who were resident with British families or in educational establishments, etc, the invalid or infirm, those who had held work permits, those who occupied key positions in essential industries, eminent scientists, research workers, etc, persons who enlisted in the Auxiliary Military Pioneer Corps, persons with sons in the British Forces, and a few other categories affecting very small numbers.'[26]

This was still not good enough for those who insisted that the list did not include those who had clearly shown themselves to be anti-Fascist. In August, therefore, a second White Paper appeared which added the notorious category 19. Aliens in this grouping were those who had shown by their writing, political activity, and such like, that they were actively friendly to Britain's interests. It was nicknamed the 'loyalty test' and, although it enlarged still further the number of aliens who could be released from internment, it also created resentment. Why should those who had committed no crime, and had no sympathy with Fascist dictatorships abroad, find themselves locked up in a camp in extremely distressing conditions merely because they could not show that they had, in the official phrase, 'taken a public and prominent part in opposition to the Nazi system'?[27]

It should be added that there was a different route altogether to release; those who 'volunteered' to join the Auxiliary Military Pioneer Corps could leave the camps and take up their new responsibilities. The response, however, was poor; by January 1941 there had been 2000 people coming forward out of a total at the time of 22 000 internees. Few were surprised at this lack of enthusiasm. After all, it was argued, it was not the best method of recruitment to lock someone up and then to say that release depended on their 'volunteering' to join the AMPC. Secondly, internees who asked for details of their projected jobs, and the conditions of service, were accused of disloyalty. Thirdly, and more worrying, aliens in the AMPC would not qualify as prisoners of war if they were captured, and they were therefore liable to be shot. Joining the Corps meant that the aliens would have to accept some of the responsibilities of British Citizenship, without enjoying its corresponding advantages.

For those who did join, there was no great spirit of welcome. One example will help to illustrate the sort of humiliation that alien recruits were made to feel. In the spring of 1942, an order was issued forbidding the use of the German language, even though this was the mother tongue of many of the aliens who had joined up. To its great credit, NCCL saw the importance of the issue; pointed out, indeed, that in the Nazi forces it was a serious offence against ideals of cultural uniformity to speak anything but German, and that in Britain we should follow rather different standards. (One can say in passing that this argument, that breaches of human rights in wartime Britain were making us 'just like the Fascists', was one that the Council used constantly.) The matter was raised with the War Office, who conceded at least that German could be spoken by the inmates when they were off duty.

Some 'friendly aliens' (especially from Belgium, Poland and

Czechoslovakia) were also detained. They could not, of course, be interned under the common law provisions, as they were not enemy aliens, so that in the event, they found themselves actually worse off. The procedure was that the Home Office issued a deportation order on selected friendly aliens, and then kept them in ordinary prisons until the distant date on which the order could be executed.

Quite apart from detention, there was another issue of central concern to aliens domiciled in Britain during the war. This was the situation brought about by the passing of the Allied Forces Act 1940. It provided, *inter alia*, that certain governments in exile (most notably the Polish one) who had military forces on British soil, would be allowed to deal with malefactors in the forces in accordance with the powers which they would have had, had they been on their native territory. Or, put another way, the British Government was to this extent conceding the right of a government in exile to exercise some judicial authority over people in Britain. NCCL consistently opposed these measures:

> Normally it is of the essence of British practice that foreigners in this country are allowed to remain beyond the jurisdiction of their own Governments, unless they have committed offences which bring them within the terms of the Extradition Acts. The emphatic view of the Council was that any measure which returned these refugees to the Authorities of the Governments from which they had fled did violence to a fundamental principle of civil liberty. The Council also pointed out that, in certain cases, of which Poland was an outstanding example, the Governments in being at the outbreak of war had not been elected by any democratic method. To give to the representatives of those Governments who had come to this country and formed provisional Governments here the powers provided by the Allied Forces Act was the negation of democracy.[28]

A particular case, which illustrated in concrete form the fears expressed thus abstractly, was that of Dr Jagodzinski. He was a lecturer in Polish at the Slavonic School of Language and, at the request of the provisional government, he was arrested by the City of London police and handed over to the Polish authorities, who detained him in their military prison in Scotland. The charge was failure to report back for duty after the expiry of leave (Dr Jagodzinski had previously served with the Polish forces). The real reason for his detention was that he was the head of a news agency which supported the government in Warsaw. A public outcry over his arrest secured his release, and indeed, in the second half of 1945, the British, Russian and American governments gave diplomatic recognition to the Warsaw regime, thus 'de-recognising' the provisional government. Jagodzinski's rescue was partly the result of his eminence; but what about the smaller fry? In April 1941, E. M. Forster, speaking on another matter (the BBC's perennial desire to suppress), remarked: 'I think we should be chiefly concerned for the smaller people. Because when important people are thrown overboard they make a big splash. We all rush to the edge and say "my goodness we must make a row". The whole affair is brought up to the front. But the smaller people don't make a spash; they vanish silently and the injustice never comes to light. We must have the greatest concern for those who have not as yet become eminent . . .'.[29]

One of the small fry who did not make the big headlines was Michulec Wladyslaw, victimised because of his support for the Warsaw government and for his desire to return home to Poland. A 26-year-old private, Wladyslaw refused to carry a rifle and cartridges, and made it clear that he did not believe in the authority of the provisional government in Britain. At this time, August 1945, his battalion was stationed near Stirling in Scotland. He was arrested and the following is an account of his experiences:

At Doune on Monday night, 13 August, he was taken to the Guard Room. There he saw a soldier struck several times, bound hand and foot, and dragged away to the stables, which are used as a place of detention. Wladyslaw was similarly dealt with. He was struck, called a 'Communist' and 'a friend of the Warsaw bandits'. Finally, a severe blow to the head rendered him unconscious. He regained consciousness in the stable, where he found himself lying bleeding profusely from the mouth and face. Four teeth from the top front row were missing. He was again kicked by the guards.

At an early hour on Tuesday morning, 14 August, he escaped from the stables and the camp and made immediately for the Doune Constabulary, which he reached about 6 am. He sought there the protective custody of the Police, who refused to extend this to him. Instead, the Police advised him to report back to his Commanding Officer, Major Kledzik. As this Major Kledzik was the officer who had ordered his beating, Private Wladyslaw chose some alternative.

Private Wladyslaw made his way to Glasgow, which he reached about noon on Wednesday 15. He was examined by a doctor in Glasgow, who provided a certificate of his condition.[30]

NCCL was very quick to organise an informal press conference. Within less than a fortnight of Wladyslaw's arrival in Glasgow, the Council had him and three other ill-treated Polish soldiers telling their stories to the journalists. These speedy responses to specific cases illustrated that, in addition to being a national organisation campaigning for a change through public debate, NCCL could also give direct assistance to individuals in trouble.

THE PRESS AND THE BBC

Right from the start, the struggle for a free press was high on the Council's agenda. In so far as the use of the Official Secrets Acts was the most notorious method of intimidating newspapers, it was not surprising that NCCL should have paid particular attention to the case of *Lewis v Cattle*. As a journalist on the *Daily Dispatch*, Lewis had, in 1937, obtained a confidential police document concerning a fraud suspect. He published an article based on the document, and this resulted in the police asking him for the name of the person who had given it him. Having refused, Lewis was found guilty by magistrates in Stockport of an offence under Section 6 of the Official Secrets Act 1920, which prohibits the withholding of information relating to an offence under the original Official Secrets Act of 1911. He was fined £5. It was an irony for Lewis, and others like him, that had he given the police what they wanted, he might have been prosecuted under Section 2 of the Official Secrets Act 1911, which penalises the possession of secret documents! The case went to appeal and the conviction was upheld.

However, day-to-day interference was manifested far more in the use of different sorts of pressure, than it was in the threat of legal sanctions. In the late 1930s, the government was afraid that its attempts at negotiation with Hitler were being undermined by anti-German sentiments in some sections of the press. (Lord Rothermere's *Daily Mail* was often pro-Fascist, and *The Times* could be relied upon not to rock the government's boat. But the *News Chronicle* and the *Manchester Guardian* were less compliant.) When the German Nazis made their protests to the British government, attempts were made to oblige them. Thus, on 8 March 1938, Dr Otto Dietrich insisted that the complete cessation of press attacks on the Nazi government was a pre-condition for negotiations with Britain. Malcolm Thompson stated that the Foreign Office then issued a request to the press 'to abstain from comments and criticisms about Germany which might impair the prospect of successful conversations. On Sunday evening, 13 March, following the annexation of Austria by Germany, the Foreign Office told the press correspondents that the ban [sic] was lifted and they could say what they liked'.[31]

Then it was Mussolini's turn. Anything which might be

offensive to the Italian dictator was severely frowned upon. At this time, a paper called the *News Review* printed extracts from a book called *Mussolini in the Making* by Gaudens Megaro, an American professor from Harvard. The Federation of London Wholesale Newsagents, which included the huge W. H. Smith chain, simply boycotted that particular issue of the paper.

Once the war had actually broken out, the issue of press censorship became the single most important preoccupation of the Council. Conferences and large public meetings were frequently being organised. The success of one of these early NCCL conferences, held at Central Hall, Westminster, on Civil Liberty and the Defeat of Fascism, on 24 August 1940, persuaded the Minister of Information, Mr Duff Cooper, to write to the Council saying that he would be pleased to meet the deputation which he had originally declined to receive. Kidd went along, of course, as did Nevinson. Allen Lane the publisher, L. C. White from the Civil Service Alliance, and Frank Owen, campaigning editor of the *Evening Standard*, were also present. At this meeting, on 7 October, Kidd presented the Minister with a memorandum detailing various abuses of the censorship regulations.

Another NCCL conference, held at Central Hall on 7 June 1941, organised in conjunction with the National Union of Journalists, was attended by over 1200 delegates, representing an aggregate membership of over $1\frac{1}{4}$ million. Another mass meeting at the same venue, on 11 April 1942, had a very distinguished panel of speakers. They included Michael Foot (then acting editor of the *Evening Standard*), Rose Macauley, Dr Joad (he of the notorious 'King and Country' debate at the Oxford Union, also of the BBC's 'Brains Trust'); members of Parliament taking part included Edith Summerskill, Aneurin Bevan and D. N. Pritt. There were smaller meetings too, such as the one organised by the Council's Press Vigilance Committee on 7 May 1942, at the Memorial Hall, Farringdon Street. This was for the editors, journalists, typists and machine workers of Fleet Street itself. Once again, Bevan was there (he was editor of *Tribune*). Tom Hopkins, editor of the

Picture Post, told the story of how indirect censorship had been exercised against his paper by the withdrawal of the vital export subsidy, and William Rust of the *Daily Worker* told of his paper's banning.

This banning of the *Daily Worker* was the most celebrated censorship case of the war. The story began on 21 June 1940, when Duff Cooper, the Minister of Information, made a startling announcement. He was wholly dissatisfied with the prevailing arrangements, under which newspapers submitted to a sort of voluntary censorship. The idea was that the papers would acquiesce in refraining from printing anything which appeared in the Defence Notices (D-Notices) which the government sent to editors, and which usually dealt with such matters as the movement and disposition of troops, the number and condition of tanks and aeroplanes, and so forth. They were also expected to consult the censors in advance if they were not sure about the publication of a particular item not covered in the Defence Notices. Although editors were not legally bound to consult the censors in this way, they found that in practice it was in their interests to do so. This was because if they published something without consultation, it might well be found to contravene one of the Defence Regulations; for example, it might be caught by 36B, prohibiting the influencing of public opinion in such a way as to be prejudicial 'to the efficient prosecution of the war'. Showing it to the censors beforehand was the sort of insurance policy against legal action that few papers could afford to neglect.

Duff Cooper's announcement was to the effect that this already tight system was to be replaced by compulsory censorship; he went on to say that the government had even toyed with the idea of having one single national paper under government control (rather like the earlier *British Gazette*) but had graciously decided to postpone this threat for the time being. Part of Duff Cooper's plan included a board of censors on which would sit six forces' personnel, one representative of the Foreign Office, one from the Ministry of Information – and one from Fleet Street! The editor of the *Evening Standard*, Frank

Owen, did not think much of the minister's plans. He called the proposed board of censors 'this incredible notion', and accused the minister of proposing 'to gag the British press. To clamp upon us here the same calamitous system of censorship which contributed so greatly to the betrayal of France'.[32]

In fact, so effective was the opposition from the press and other libertarians that within a very short time the Prime Minister found himself having to give a personal assurance that the voluntary system would remain in effect. But, although this represented something of a victory, the censors still had sharp teeth. The *Daily Worker* was told that the opinions contained in it were unacceptable to the authorities; and in early 1941 it was suppressed, under Defence Regulation 2D. This regulation, which had been introduced in the previous year, allowed the authorities to prohibit any newspaper which systematically published opinions which might foment opposition to the war. There was not much argument about the substance of the charge; protests were directed against the use of 2D at all. The ban was on the front cover of *Civil Liberty* for February, with Kidd waxing eloquent:

> I say it is an almost intolerable strain that is imposed upon staunch and independent democrats. We find the Government and their supporters of many kinds, prating that while they suppress an unpopular minority newspaper they are deeply concerned for 'the real' freedom of the Press! Always they disapprove of repression until the time comes when they find they want to repress their political opponents. But that has been the technique of religious and political intolerance throughout history – the profession of liberal and humanitarian sentiments accompanied by drastic repression or persecution, always on the grounds that the particular person who is the object of the attack is not 'genuine', is not 'honest' in his views, is a 'disloyalist' or a 'freethinker'. Take all the rebels of history from Joan of Arc to Bradlaugh. Think how they were repressed by exactly the same excuses of urgent necessity as are advanced today. . . . What is Mr

Herbert Morrison's excuse but a repetition of a plea of State necessity, by which plea Hitler and Mussolini have sought to justify their own repressions.[33]

I quote at such length because Kidd has here advanced part of the classic case for an absolute freedom to publish. The opposite case was put with considerable force by (ironically) another NCCL luminary, D. N. Pritt. Pritt, in the early years of the post-war Labour Government under Atlee, was disgusted by what he saw as the favouritism and protection afforded to Fascists by the Home Office, through their lenient interpretation of the provisions of the Public Order Act 1936, which, it will be remembered, was originally conceived as a specifically anti-Blackshirt measure. Pritt's argument was that legislation needed to be introduced to forbid the advocacy of Fascist ideas, and his reasoning was simply that 'We are all – or nearly all – satisfied that the public advocacy of Fascism at this stage of history is wholly inexcusable'[34] and that the problem was to devise legislation to ensnare the Fascists which did not rebound on their enemies. To him, Kidd's position was untenable: 'The "liberal" argument that everyone – including Fascists – should have freedom of propaganda attracted a good many people who did not realise that the cause of freedom of speech is not served, but gravely endangered, if such freedom be conceded to those who intend to use it to destroy freedom of speech for everybody, as the Fascist sought to do.'[35]

On the one hand, Kidd does not rely on arguments against suppression so much as denunciations of the hypocrisy of those who make fake distinctions. Pritt, on the other hand, simply takes it for granted that freedom of speech should be taken away from those hostile to others' freedom. It is a debate which continues within NCCL to this day.

Whether any of Kidd's arguments had any force in Whitehall is open to doubt. But in the event, the ban on the *Daily Worker* was lifted in the summer of 1942, and the Council put out a statement welcoming the move.

It is worth noting in passing that the spectre of censorship clearly made the editor of *Civil Liberty* circumspect, for we find here and there accounts of events from which names, dates and locations have been excluded! For example: 'On one occasion, in a big town, a representative of the Legal Department of the National Council for Civil Liberties had an interview with the Chief Constable and the organiser . . .'.[36]

The BBC also gave trouble. Late in 1940, it told an employee that once he had registered as a conscientious objector, he would be dismissed. The corporation was also antagonistic to the People's Convention Movement, which had been set up to engage with civil liberty issues (particularly as they affected the working class) by means of 'vigilance' committees operating in local districts. Industrial disputes and the provision of social services were amongst the topics of concern to the PCM. Supporters of the PCM and similar 'left' organisations soon found themselves banned from the airwaves. Although technicians, clergymen, announcers, script-writers and administrators were among those 'purged', it was the banning of two musicians (Alan Bush and Sir Hugh Robertson) which created the greatest furore.

The public outcry at the bans was loud and long. The actor Michael Redgrave, speaking at a public meeting organised by NCCL, told how he was summoned to the BBC offices to be questioned about his political views, and refused to discuss them; he simply, in his own words, 'banned himself'.[37] Vaughan Williams, the musician, wrote to *The Times* informing its readers that he was withdrawing from a commission to compose a choral song and was returning his fee to the corporation. E. M. Forster followed suit, pulling out of two forthcoming broadcasts on India and the empire. As Prime Minister, Churchill had to fend off awkward questions on the bans from irate members of the House of Commons. Eventually, the policy of banning conscientious objectors, pacifists, Communists, and dissidents in general, was abandoned. Pressure against it was too great; and the reconstitution of the board of governors must have played a significant part in this change of heart.

At the outbreak of war, all but two of the governors were sacked. The two who remained (Sir Allan Powell and Captain C. Millis) could be relied upon to implement the government's wishes in regard to broadcasting without asking awkward questions. There was not much protest from amongst those dismissed, with the honourable exception of Dr H. A. L. Fisher. Then, in March 1941, at the height of the controversy over the bans, the Minister of Information, Duff Cooper, announced that two government advisors had been appointed to the BBC; he conceded that they would 'no doubt increase the control exercised by the Government'.[38] Churchill was clearly more libertarian on this issue than Duff Cooper, and only a few weeks after the announcement about the advisors, the board of governors was reconstituted. Ronald Kidd described this as 'another triumph for Mr Churchill's good sense and our campaign', and went on to conclude that 'the BBC cannot expect us to have the slightest confidence in its wisdom or in its good faith if it attempts to return to the methods of petty persecution which the Prime Minister has condemned'.[39]

3   1946–59

COURTS MARTIAL AND THE ARMED FORCES

There was a widely-held view throughout the war that the nature of the forces – the snobbery and class-based élitism in particular – had to be changed. The old style was bad enough in peace time when all soldiers were volunteers, but with wartime conscription it was felt to be intolerable that men should not only have to make the sacrifice of serving under compulsion during the best years of their life, but that they also had to experience the humiliating restraints imposed by antiquated conventions and regulations. It was by no means only a question of social division, although throughout the war NCCL recorded many instances of officers instructing the staffs of bars and hotels not to admit their men, and even cases of officers insisting that other ranks actually leave restaurants, for example, if the officers wished to use them. There were complaints more serious than this, and one of them was that the troops were not sufficiently encouraged to think for themselves on weighty matters of the day, but instead treated as hopeless blockheads.

A notorious demonstration of this attitude had occurred during the war itself when the military authorities reacted with such hostility to the so-called Cairo Parliament. The Parliament was a kind of debating club but with members elected on party political lines, as at Westminster. It was only after the Parliament elections, when Labour members outnumbered Conservatives by five to one, that the British military authorities in Egypt began to suppress the whole venture.

Military police attended the debates, the organisers were threatened with King's Regulation 541 (prohibiting soldiers from participating in politics), and key figures (such as Aircraftman Leo Abse, later to become a member of the Westminster Parliament) were suddenly posted elsewhere. D. N. Pritt agitated in England in an attempt to restrain the repressive zeal of the authorities in Cairo; but in this instance he was without success. The Parliament was effectively killed off. Pritt described the whole affair in these terms: 'It is a classic illustration of unteachable reaction, untruthfulness, stupidity, and incompetence on the part of the Army authorities . . .'.[1] NCCL felt that the events in Egypt were sufficiently important in terms of their implications for the civil liberties of service personnel to warrant the publication of a booklet, written by R. J. Spector, telling the full story of the Cairo Parliament.[2]

It was against this sort of background that the Attwood case occurred. The events took place at an RAF camp in Karachi in January of 1946 and can be told in Aircraftman Attwood's own words:

For many months feeling boiled over on the question of demobilisation; there was dissatisfaction on this subject and also over the disparity between the releases of trades and lack of news, and this was further aggravated by vile conditions at the camp: atrocious food, excessive overtime, and an increase in disciplinary standards, which were mounting precisely because of the failure of existing machinery for airing grievances. The lid finally blew off, there were a few mass meetings, telephone wires between Delhi and London grew hot, and the Commodore arrived. We elected our delegation and laid our complaints before him.

Only two days before our delegation met the Air Commodore, the commanding officer of our unit refused our request to reduce the hours, giving excuses why we should be content to work long hours. Following our delegation, however, there was a tremendous transformation in the camp, the hours were suddenly reduced, and we achieved not a 40-hour week but a 36-hour week. Large sections of the camp had lived in tents, which were literally falling apart, because of long years' exposure, and we had tried many times to get them repaired or changed. Now, overnight, new tents sprang up like mushrooms, officers were instructed to fraternise with the men – and some of them even did it! Seats appeared in the airmen's canteens, easy chairs and carpets were installed. Kit inspections were cancelled, and food made so remarkable that men began to complain about too much to eat. Demobilisation was speeded up, news was given out regularly, and complaints were looked into . . .[3]

It all seemed too good to be true, and of course it was. Two months later, Attwood, who had in the meantime been elected chairman of a grievance committee, was arrested. He was placed in solitary confinement and charged with mutiny, for which one of the penalties was capital punishment. This was despite the fact that on at least three earlier occasions, the airmen had been assured that there would be no victimisation as a result of the series of protests that had taken place.

The authorities made every effort to frustrate Attwood's defence; one of their methods was to delay his mail. Registered letters which Attwood sent to two MPs, Pritt and Tom Driberg, were held back for over a week. Attempts to communicate with some lawyers in India were so delayed that Attwood heard from them only after the trial was over. A letter from the Electrical Trades Union, to Attwood, was returned, having been marked 'Whereabouts unknown'.

In a series of bizarre twists, Attwood was initially found innocent, re-tried on the same charge and found guilty, and finally had the guilty verdict quashed, with no reason being given, by the military authorities! NCCL gave its support to a special group which had been set up in May of 1946 (called the Attwood and Other Services Defence Committee) to pay off the outstanding legal expenses of the case (only £300 of the full bill of £1000 had so far been subscribed), and to secure 'the support of all Trade Union and Socialist bodies for the future democratisation of the Services, and to set up constitutional machinery within the Services in order that all other ranks can air their grievances in a constitutional manner'.[4]

Attwood was a guest speaker at an NCCL meeting held on 10 November at the Palace Theatre, London, the purpose of which was to discuss democratic rights in the armed forces and to launch a campaign on the vital issues. A future Labour Prime Minister, Lt. J. Callaghan, also spoke. Both men stressed the need for the authorities to recognise the rights of forces personnel to collective representation. The meeting decided on the priorities which NCCL should adopt, which were as follows: full political and civil rights for the armed forces; the revision of military law, especially courts martial and the use of summary punishments; better educational provision and vocational training; and the right to free voluntary association. It is a measure of the importance which the Council attached to this issue that it set up a special 'Sub-Committee of Forces Freedom' which later merged with the Attwood committee.

As a result of pressure from NCCL and other bodies, a government committee under Mr Justice Lewis was formed in November 1946, to review courts martial procedures. The Lewis Committee reported in 1949, and recommended a reduction in delays in administering military justice; legal aid facilities for the accused; a system of appeals against conviction by a court martial; new procedural rules; and the transfer of military justice from the ranks of serving officers to independent Judges Martial. Neil Lawson, who held the chair of the Council's Forces' sub-committee, welcomed the recommendations but felt that they did not go far enough. The navy would not be affected at all by the Lewis proposals; more seriously, the view that only officers should serve on courts martial was reaffirmed. Lawson, who cited the example of the American forces, which were then endeavouring to introduce 'other ranks' into the administration of justice, noted that the British system was antiquated: 'the citizen soldiers who comprised the bulk of the armed forces during the last war, will have their own view on this matter'.[5] At the Council's AGM held on 9 April 1949, a resolution proposed by the executive committee urging access for 'other ranks' to the courts martial, and calling for parallel legislation for all three services, was passed. In 1950, an almost identical motion was passed at the AGM.

The Lewis proposal of having Judges Martial was never implemented, but a separate legal aid system for accused persons in the services was introduced, as was a right of appeal from a court martial to the higher civil courts.

FREEDOM OF EXPRESSION

In view of its experiences with the BBC during the war, it was not surprising that, once the peace came, NCCL devoted a great deal of energy attempting to reform the corporation and make it answerable for its actions. The basic argument was that, bearing in mind the enormous power that a broadcasting monopoly entailed, it was quite improper for the BBC to derive its legitimacy from a Royal Charter of 1926, when it should be accountable to Parliament. It was (and is) true that the government of the day had an absolute right of veto over all BBC matters, including the power to order the withdrawal of programmes felt to be too sensitive or controversial. However, Parliament itself had no direct powers of scrutiny, and this was the Council's complaint.

There were other structural problems too. The BBC was too centralised in London, and its managers had no idea of, or contact with, the majority of citizens; a point which had been made by the Ullswater Committee in 1936. But what chiefly engaged the attention of NCCL was the specific acts of censorship and suppression. There was no shortage of people to come forward to tell their experiences: the comedian Ronald Frankau explained how his jokes had been politically vetoed, Tom Driberg MP told in *Reynold's News*[6] of his being dropped as a contributor because of his failure to conform to corporation policy, and the writer Francis Williams gave an account of the methods used to 'persuade' him to a particular view. In 1946, an American journalist from CBS called Howard Smith prepared a BBC broadcast on the Foreign Secretaries' Conference. It was felt that Smith's talk was insufficiently critical of the Soviet Union, and too hostile to Western countries; it was banned by the BBC. The official reason given was that Smith had not provided 'a balanced account of American opinion'.[7] In addition to all this there was, of course, the famous 'blacklist'.

The conditions under which BBC staff were hired grievously infringed basic civil liberties, including freedom of expression. For example, one regulation governing conditions of service prohibited 'any action likely to attract publicity or to cause controversy'.[8] No member of staff was permitted to engage in politics, even at the local level, without permission.

A second way in which freedom of expression was restricted in this period manifested itself in the post-war anti-Communist hysteria. On 15 March 1948, the Prime Minister, Clement Attlee, announced in the Commons that, because membership of the Communist Party might be inimical to the aims of the state in some cases, it had been decided that members of the Party, and all those associated with it 'in such a way as to raise legitimate doubts about his or her reliability'[9] would be removed from Civil Service posts concerned with the security of the state; an effort would be made to find them alternative posts in non-sensitive areas, but failing this they would be dismissed outright. It was assumed at the time that, because no domestic scandal or incident had occurred to lead to Attlee's statement, it must have been made as a result of pressure from Washington – by this time, the American Congress's Committee on Un-American Activities was notorious.

Of course, the principle involved in the purge was especially invidious because it was being openly acknowledged that there was a danger of disloyalty from only some Communists, and that all were being penalised simply on the grounds of the practical difficulty of separating the loyal from the potentially

disloyal; in other words, the government accepted all along that
innocent people would suffer great hardship as a consequence
of expediency rather than natural justice. Furthermore, despite
the assurance that the purge would be confined only to those in
sensitive posts dealing with security matters, it was in fact
applied across the board to all posts in the Supply and Service
Ministries.

Communist Party meetings were constantly being harassed.
In Herne Bay in 1949, the Party had been told by the local
police that if they wished to hold a meeting (it was at a regular
meeting place on the highway) they would need permission
from the district council. When applied for, this was refused.
However, an astute holiday-maker, Mr Butter, President of the
Westminster Trades Council and a member of NCCL, contacted the Council and told it of these developments. The
Council sent a letter to the Herne Bay authorities pointing out
that there was no law which allowed local councils to control
public meetings of this sort. The Herne Bay Council then
received a deputation from the meeting's organisers which Mr
Butter also attended. At this meeting, the delegation declared
after lengthy discussion that the proposed meeting would go
ahead whether the local council liked it or not. In the event,
when the evening of the meeting arrived, no attempt was made
by the police to disperse the crowd. Extraordinarily, however,
just before the meeting began, a policeman approached the
speaker and told him that he was to refrain from mentioning the
discussion which had taken place between the deputation and
the District Council. Mr Butter, luckily on hand again,
challenged the police there and then on this matter; he said that
he would advise the speaker that he should say what he liked,
and not brook any attempt by the police to exceed their
authority, as they were patently doing on this occasion. The
speaker was finally able to say what he had come to say; and
thus two examples of overweening and improper use of the
power conferred by authority were successfully overthrown by
the vigilance of a challenger.

Members of the Communist Party in Grimsby also ran into

trouble with the police: two of them were charged with obstructing police officers and obstructing the highway. NCCL's *Annual Report* for 1949–50 also mentions cases in Hornchurch and Hackney in which the hiring of sites and premises to the local Trades Councils was refused on political grounds. But the event which most clearly illustrated the tenacity of anti-Communist sentiment in the highest reaches of government was the sabotaging of the Sheffield Peace Conference, which was to have taken place in the early part of November 1950. It was organised by a pro-Soviet group called 'Partisans of Peace' and many delegates had been invited to attend from Eastern Europe. Whilst both Attlee and his Home Secretary, Ede, looked upon the conference with extreme disfavour, they declared in the Commons in October that their intervention would be confined to refusing entry visas only to those who could be classed as *persona non grata*, a category normally reserved for known criminals, persons hostile to the best interests of the British state, and the like. Ede actually boasted of what he took to be Britain's superiority over Communist countries in precisely this matter of allowing free movement and debate: '. . . we still have some prestige in the world because we have remained a country of freedom and are not afraid of people seeing how we are living'.[10] Both Attlee and Ede gave assurances that they would not jeopardise Britain's reputation as a country of free speech.

However, once the delegates started arriving, visas were refused wholesale. Almost every one of the World Peace Committee was denied entry. Permission for eighteen charter flights from Prague, which had been organised to bring the Czech delegates, was rescinded. The Congress had to be cancelled. That Ede had departed from his stated intention of excluding only those who were undesirable as individuals (as opposed to being undesirable on account of the purpose of their visit) was blatantly clear. It could be seen in the case of the delegate who wished to visit the Congress and then, immediately afterwards, attend a meeting of the Council of the International Association of Democratic Lawyers. He was allowed to attend the lawyers' meeting, but not the Congress. Even those unsympathetic to the 'Partisans of Peace' group were outraged at the government's behaviour. The general secretary of the Tobacco Workers' Union, Percy Belcher, caught the sentiments of very many people:

> We, in this country, have always boasted of our long tradition of tolerance for other people's views on all subjects and our willingness to grant freedom of speech to all and sundry, and this latest move by the Government is, in my opinion, one which should call for the strongest protest from all who seek for better understanding in our international relationships.
>
> As one whose life has been spent in the working class movement I cannot but feel that such an attitude is only playing into the hands of those reactionary forces who seek to impose their way of life on others and who, without regard to our traditions of democracy, are using the Communist bogy to introduce what is tantamount to an era of unbridled Fascism under the guise of freedom.[11]

In January 1949, an anonymous contributor to *Civil Liberty* began a piece on the Fascist threat with the following sentiment: 'The right of freedom of speech has always implied the acceptance of responsibility. It has never been seriously suggested that this right should include a licence to such things as real incitement, indecency or libel. It is, therefore, all the more remarkable that so little is being done by responsible authorities to check those who are today demanding not liberty but licence.'[12] It was the Pritt–Kidd argument all over again – indeed, it goes on still, in NCCL and outside it – about whether an absolute freedom could, more importantly should, exist. And if, with Pritt, you wanted to draw a line, then who would draw it and using what criteria?

The circumstances surrounding E. M. Forster's resignation from membership of NCCL, in 1948, seem to me to be very much to do with 'drawing lines' in this sense. Forster, of course, had been NCCL's first president; he had given up the post before the war, partly because of ill-health. When Attlee's Communist purge was at its height, in 1948, the Council's AGM debated a censure motion. Forster had already had trouble in the 1930s fending off criticism that NCCL was a front organisation for the Communists. In 1935, when NCCL was drafting a declaration of principles, Forster managed to change the wording of a clause which, in its original form, spoke of the threat to civil liberties 'from whatever quarter'. Forster's version – 'the threat from left or right'[13] – demonstrated his concern to ensure that the Council remained non-party political, and also hinted at his reservations about Communist members. He was publicly accused of naïvety about their influence. In addition, he had never tried to hide his dislike of Communism: 'It would destroy nearly everything I understand and like, and I want the present economic and social order to continue.'[14] Friends like Leonard Woolf warned him about the Communist influence in NCCL. He was, for these reasons, in a mood to defect. He did so, and announced the reasons in the *New Statesman*:

Sir,
Perhaps you will allow me to state in your columns that I have resigned my membership of the National Council for Civil Liberties.

I have done so on account of the putting forward of an emergency resolution at the annual general meeting last March. The resolution in question invited the meeting to censure the Government for its proposed purge of Communists in key positions. The chairman, when introducing it on behalf of the executive, indicated that it was a civil liberties resolution, and therefore appropriate. I cannot agree. It seems to me that it was essentially a political resolution, and that, since the Council is a non-party body, it should not have been put . . .[15]

The letter was unconvincing for at least two reasons. In the first place, Forster, as we have seen, took a prominent role in opposing the ban on Communists imposed during the war by the BBC, and his letter thus seemed to renege on his earlier, principled, stand. Secondly, the issue could be seen as *both* party-political and of concern to libertarians. The distinction is difficult to draw, and in the 1980s it is still troublesome. (Motions at recent AGMs have been excluded on grounds of being party-political, but there is a substantial body of opinion which believes that individual political parties could and should be censured in motions when and if their policies transgress NCCL principles).

Forster's qualms are not, in themselves, of great moment. But in so far as they reflect the unease experienced by those who reject notions of 'absolute principle' as spurious, they illustrate a central dilemma of NCCL itself: how to claim validity, how to support intellectually, the position adopted once lines have been drawn; and how to rebut claims that the line-drawing is merely arbitrary and subjective.

MENTAL HEALTH

One of NCCL's great successes was its role in campaigning against the antiquated Mental Deficiency Act of 1913 and seeing it replaced by the Mental Health Act 1959. Under the earlier law, people could be classified as 'mentally deficient' on grounds which today sound fantastic; they included the sexually promiscuous ('moral defectives') and those who, in their families, were 'neglected, abandoned, without visible means of support, or cruelly treated . . .'. Wide powers existed under the Act to detain such people for unspecified periods; the only real curb was that the 'deficiency' had to have manifested itself before the eighteenth birthday of the person concerned. The system was run by a Board of Control, which was able to wield its powers without being properly accountable either to Parliament or to the Minister of Health.

In 1947, the Council's attention was drawn to the case of 'Jane' who, as a result of having given birth to an illegitimate child and refused shelter by her father, was detained. A cousin attempted to have Jane released into her care, but the Health Committee refused this application on the grounds that the cousin's home was unsuitable. This was in spite of the recommendation of the Lunacy Commissioners that Jane's detention in a senile ward was deplorable and that she should be released. NCCL began *habeas corpus* proceedings, and Jane was quickly freed. Later in the year, *Civil Liberty* noted that in similar cases, 'release has sometimes been rapidly given when serious enquiries have been initiated'.[16]

A more notorious case, and one described in an article ironically entitled 'This Modern Age', concerned another woman also called Jane. In March 1945, she appeared before a Juvenile Court as a person in need of care and protection, following the prosecution of her mother. The court also heard that she had been backward at school. These two facts led the court to order her detention, even though her parents did not consent. (Under the 1913 Act, such consent was unnecessary where it was felt that it had been 'unreasonably withheld'.) In August 1946, she was sent out as a domestic worker in a local convent where she received 16s 8d per week, plus board and keep. Later, she was transferred to a convent and mental institution in the London area. Here she worked under a very strict regime in a commercial laundry for 1s per week in wages:

Jane says that she worked in the Packing Room of the Laundry for the first six months of her stay there. Along with the other girls, she tells us, she had to rise each day at 6.30 am, attend Mass at 7 am, and commence her duties in the laundry at 8 am. Half an hour was allowed for lunch, followed by Thanksgiving at 1 pm. Work was then resumed until 5.30 pm. At 6 pm there was a third church service, followed by supper at 7 pm – then the girls were immediately sent to bed. She added that on Saturday the girls worked from 8 am to 1 pm; in the afternoon they had to do PT. After tea they were free. On Sunday, they had to attend church twice. On very rare occasions they were taken out to the pictures by the nuns, and on other occasions some of them were taken out for walks under supervision.[17]

In March 1949, Jane ran away to her parents' home. A week later, four policemen and a policewoman caught up with her. She spent the night in a cell and was then taken back to the laundry. In September, she ran away again and this time managed to keep clear of the authorities. Some friends contacted a Legal Advice Bureau and brought in NCCL. Independent medical opinion was sought. Early in November, Jane was given a complete examination by a psychiatrist who came to the conclusion that although she was backward, she was not 'mentally defective'. NCCL passed this information on to the Board of Control and advised them that the girl had agreed to return to the institution but an application for Jane's discharge would be submitted. This was successful and Jane was completely free within a month.

Jane was lucky in that she was able to make a new life for herself whilst still only nineteen. Others were not so fortunate. May was sixteen at the end of the First World War when she was found staying out late with soldiers. She was detained. Her wage during her period of employment in the institution amounted to 6d per week. She was released on licence twice to work as a domestic servant in another hospital. Once, the licence was revoked because she wrote a note to a male friend. On a second occasion, it was revoked because a girl released at the same time as May, and working in the same hospital, was pregnant. The authorities stated that 'we naturally did not want other disasters, and although May is 45 years of age, she is not beyond the age of child-bearing'.[18] Much later, in the discussions for reform that preceded the report of the Royal Commission on Mental Health (published in May 1957), this question of relationships with the opposite sex was taken up fully. The Minister of Health claimed that: 'The Statutory Regulations do not require it to be a condition of licence in every case that the patient should not be allowed to form attachments with the opposite sex.'[19] NCCL knew otherwise: 'This statement is completely false. The statutory form contains precisely the provision quoted and Regulation 7 demands the application of that form to all cases.'[20]

The cases of Jane and May were two out of twelve presented to a special NCCL Conference on Mental Deficiency held on 10 June 1950. Also cited was the case of Betty, seized under the Act three days before the wedding which would have legitimised her child; and William, a tuberculosis sufferer, who was held for two years under a Mental Deficiency Order despite his IQ score of 107. All cases showed evidence of exploitation, with full-time employment being rewarded with wages ranging from 6d to 5s per week. It was also apparent in most of the cases that recourse to the Act was not the result of a long period of studying the mental capabilities of the individuals concerned, but rather the result of some outside circumstance such as the prosecution of a mother, complaints about a child's behaviour, or merely running away. Generally, the circumstances leading to certification occurred in early or middle adolescence, when most youngsters find themselves in some sort of trouble. Finally, it was pointed out that parents or relatives were given no opportunity to challenge the evidence presented in reports to judicial authorities before certification.

The Conference regretted that lengthy campaigns were necessary before cases were reviewed. Visiting Committees were criticised for failing to inform parents of their rights. Changed home circumstances, the existence of means of care and protection outside institutions, proof that work and behaviour on licence were satisfactory – none of these considerations seemed able to secure a discharge. The onus was on patients or relatives to obtain psychiatric evidence that there was actually no deficiency. Needless to say, parents who were unable to afford the expense of a private psychiatrist found it almost impossible to get mental deficiency orders discharged. The Conference made a number of proposals which included: the abolition of the sub-category 'moral defective'; certification to be made by two doctors, one of whom at least should be a qualified psychiatrist; the establishing of a right of appeal against all orders made and against decisions that parental consent was unreasonably withheld; and the annual review, by independent psychiatrists, of the cases of all 'high-grade mental defectives'.

Hard on the heels of the Conference came the publication of NCCL's forthright pamphlet *55,000 Outside the Law*, which came out early in 1951. It claimed that five out of six cases did not involve mental deficiency at all, properly speaking; that legal safeguards were inadequate, especially in the area of parental consent; and that there was exploitation of the work done by the detained. (Later, the Council drew attention to an extract from the Wood Report of 1929, which explained how it was that mental institutions have a vested interest in retaining patients: 'An institution which takes all types and ages is economical because the high-grade patients do the work and make everything necessary, not only for themselves, but for the lower grade. In an institution taking only low grades, the whole of the work has to be done by paid staff.'[21])

The pamphlet was very well received by the press:

– 'The document . . . exposes the Dickensian ideas that govern the lives of these unfortunate young men and women.' (*Reynold's News*)

– 'In its best tradition, the National Council for Civil Liberties has done a great service to some of our weaker citizens.' (*Public Opinion*)

– 'Mentally weak are exploited, they say.' (*Daily Mirror*)

– 'So startling, so well authenticated, is the staggering document that nothing less than a full-scale public enquiry will satisfy any humane person.' (*Sunday Pictorial*)

– '. . . the cases quoted – which they say are only a representative few out of 200 which have already been brought to their notice – are sufficiently disturbing to indicate that a full enquiry into the present administration of the mental-deficiency services would not be amiss.' (*The Lancet*)

The *Medical World* carried a three-page review and a leading article entitled 'Lesser Breeds Without the Law'. It referred to the Mental Deficiency Service 'governed and stultified by absurdly anachronistic and completely unrealistic concepts, laws and organisation.'[22]

The campaign was snowballing. The Council called a second conference on the Mental Deficiency laws, held in the summer of 1951. In 1953, the Prime Minister gave in to the pressure and announced that there would be a Royal Commission to investigate the workings of the law. Before it could report, the most famous of the cases taken up by the Council had hit the headlines.

Kathleen Rutty had been placed in an orphanage at three months, and from that time until her seventeenth birthday she had been shunted from one institution to another. At that point she was transferred from a local authority hostel to a mental institution under a 'place of safety' order. The order was made without the obligatory examination by a magistrate, and was therefore illegal; but this only came to light after Kathleen had spent seven years illegally detained. NCCL successfully brought *habeas corpus* proceedings in the High Court. Lord Goddard, the Lord Chief Justice, was extremely critical of those administering the 1913 law: 'There are plenty of idle, naughty and mischievous children and young persons who are not mental defectives within the meaning of the Act . . . it is of first importance that the judicial authority should not think he is merely to act as a rubber stamp . . . persons of whatever age are not intended to be deprived of their liberty and confined to an institution merely because doctors and officials think it would be good for them.'[23]

The result of the Rutty judgement was that the Ministry of

Health stated that patients who had completed twelve months out on licence would be released unless there was an overwhelming objection to this course. The publicity involved in the Rutty case also resulted in the Council being inundated with hundreds of similar cases; and the campaign in Parliament gathered in strength.

The Royal Commission reported in May, 1957. It was a blistering attack on the whole system: the ban on sexual association, the censorship of mail, and the absence of a scheme for voluntary patients. And there was another case. A Labour MP, Tom Williams, linked up with the Council over the plight of Peter Whitehead, who had been illegally detained at Rampton. They began legal proceedings and this was enough to secure Whitehead's release. The authorities were running scared. They released 800 people in 1957 and a further 1000 in the following year – it was a heady bonanza of freedom.

In 1959, the Mental Health Act, based on the findings of the Royal Commission, was passed. The Act of 1913 was abolished, together with the Board of Control; voluntary admissions to mental institutions were made possible; the idea of 'moral defectiveness', which had no place in medical terminology, was abandoned; those detained would have to be released automatically on reaching the age of 25 unless they were dangerous; above all, a mental health review tribunal, with at least one lay member, was set up to hear appeals from patients against their detention.

The Council's response was to establish a large team of volunteers ready to act for patients at these tribunals. After five years of the working of the Act, NCCL had won about half of the cases that it had taken up in this way.

The man responsible for coordinating NCCL's work in the years leading up to the passing of the Act, died in February 1959. Frank Haskell was head of the Council's Mental Deficiency Department, having joined the NCCL staff soon after the war. Like Kidd, he suffered from chronic ill health, and like Kidd, he refused to let that interfere with his commitment to the work. It was a sad irony that he should not live to see the passage of the legislation that he did so much to bring about. On his death, the Council set up a fund in his memory.

The significance of the Council's work in the area of mental health is well summarised by Barry Cox:

> The legislation was one of the most impressive of the NCCL's achievements. From its accidental discovery of the injustice in 1947, the NCCL had masterminded the campaign for reform of the law and had handled nearly a thousand individual cases, creating legal history as it did so. It had been handsomely supported in this by most of the press, though not . . . by the BBC. The campaign had also brought about a major change in the attitudes of those running the institutions themselves.[24]

4 1960–74

RACE RELATIONS AND IMMIGRATION

Elizabeth Allen's successor as general secretary of the Council, Martin Ennals, took up his post in 1960. One of his special interests was the fight against racism, and in this of course he was following a well-established NCCL tradition, evident, for example, both in the Council's work on colonial matters, and also in its vigorous opposition to the 'colour bar' in the 1950s. Ennals helped ensure, for example, that the Council supported Fenner Brockway MP in his repeated attempts to introduce legislation to make racial discrimination and incitement to racial hatred a criminal offence. Brockway's Bill was especially concerned with discrimination by hoteliers and pub landlords, for it was in these cases in particular that overt discrimination had come to public attention.

For example, in 1963 the Balham United Services Club put up a notice in its premises telling members that black guests were not to be brought to the club. One of the club members, Mr Tilley, alerted the Council to the situation. In the meantime, the Working Men's Club and Institute Union, to which the Balham club was affiliated, issued a statement refusing 'to persuade any Club to admit or debar' potential guests, such matters being 'entirely for each individual Club Committee in its discretion to decide in the best interests of the Club and its members'.[1] In 1964, the George pub in Herne Hill, South London, operated a 'colour bar' in its saloon. There was a protest picket outside the pub, and some of the demonstrators were arrested and charged with obstruction, and with using

82

threatening words and behaviour. In this case, NCCL arranged legal representation for the defendants, who were acquitted.

Later in the year, an anti-racist group held a sit-in at the Dartmouth Arms in Forest Hill, followed by a picket; at one stage, the police present assisted the landlord in turning away a West Indian who was attempting to enter. The Council decided to pursue the legal implications of this action, and wrote to the Metropolitan Police Commissioner, suggesting that, although the law might allow police to assist with the removal of trespassers in such circumstances, it did not place a *duty* on them to do so. In view of this, would the Commissioner agree to a meeting with NCCL to discuss their policy. No, the Commissioner did not feel able to agree to such a meeting. In Leicester, another pub sit-in resulted in the usual crop of obstruction and assault charges against protesters. NCCL urged people to use the magistrates' courts to oppose licence renewals for such pubs, but this approach did not prove to be successful.

Employment was another crucial issue. The Bristol authorities excluded black people from employment on their buses, arguing that there was 'already a white waiting list, coloured recruitment would mean an exodus of white staff, coloured busmen in London are rude and arrogant'.[2] In the event, Bristol removed the ban after a storm of publicity. Another issue – then as now – was the scarcity of black policemen. At that time, although senior police chiefs had no openly-admitted policy of exclusion, the Police Federation were publicly saying in this period that they were opposed to the recruitment of blacks.

In 1965, an attempt was made to call a halt to the increasing manifestations of racism. The Race Relations Act was passed, and its main provisions were as follows: a prohibition on racial discrimination in places of public resort; a ban on tenancy restrictions on racial grounds; penalising any act which constituted incitement to racial hatred; and an amendment to the Public Order Act 1936 whereby written matter (speech was already covered) could be the subject of a prosecution if it were to be found so threatening or abusive as to be intended to cause, or likely to cause, a breach of the peace. The Act set up a conciliation machinery which would have to be used before the parties could have access to the courts. Finally, a Race Relations Board was established, chaired by Mark Bonham-Carter.

The Council had very serious reservations about the Act; the main complaint was that it did not go far enough, and did not have enough teeth. For example, the prohibition on discrimination only applied to public places, which NCCL found particularly unfortunate: 'Anything not included is therefore excluded and may be considered as permitting discrimination in housing, employment, insurance, credit facilities, private boarding houses, holiday tours, etc.'[3]

The Council had very serious reservations about the Act; the toughening of the law; and indeed, in 1976, there was another Race Relations Act which did just that. But just as Chaucer told us 600 years ago that 'love knoweth no laws', it has always been clear that hate shares the same distinction. The strictest rules would not prevent the sort of racist attacks which representatives from the Standing Conference of West Indian organisations complained of at the Home Office, after the passing of the Act:

> . . . just before Christmas a coloured man . . . was assaulted so severely that he had to have 60 stitches in his head. There have been reports of incidents in West London and South London where coloured people walking along the street have been shot at from passing cars with air-guns. Many West Indians feel that they are not receiving adequate police protection: and Pakistanis and Indians have the same apprehension, especially after two incidents in Southall, one relating to a burglary at an Indian's home and the other to an assault in a public house. In both cases the police were not anxious to take action. On Christmas Day a Pakistani law student, serving as a waiter during the vacation, was

attacked by four men in a restaurant in Liverpool. He lost three teeth and was bleeding profusely when the police arrived on the scene. However, the men concerned were not detained.[4]

In June, 1968, NCCL organised an emergency 'Speak-Out on Race' meeting at the Friends' Meeting House in Euston Road, London. It was part of a campaign which was mounted largely in response to the notorious 'rivers of blood' speech delivered by Enoch Powell in April. The Annual Report speaks of Powell's views in the following vein: 'April 1968 was perhaps the cruellest month for race relations ever experienced in Britain.'[5] Despite a British Rail work-to-rule, 500 managed to attend, and speeches were made by, amongst others, Joan Lestor, MP, Peggy Ashcroft, Des Wilson (then with Shelter), Sam Silkin, MP, and Martin Ennals, who had left NCCL in 1966 to take a job with the National Committee for Commonwealth Immigrants. The meeting was followed up in December by a visit to the Home Secretary, James Callaghan, at which NCCL's general secretary, Tony Smythe, presented the 'Speak-Out Declaration on Race', with thousands of signatures.

In September 1969, judgement was given in the very first case brought under the Race Relations Act. A building firm in Huddersfield had refused to sell one of its houses to Mr Mahesh Uphadhyaya; the Race Relations Board had investigated the matter, and then contacted the firm, setting out the terms of a proposed settlement: namely, an apology from the firm for the humiliation suffered by the complainant, and an offer to sell him a house. The company refused this settlement, nor would it give an undertaking to refrain from such discriminatory practices in future. The case went to the Leeds County Court, which found that there had indeed been unlawful discrimination under the Act. However, owing to a technicality – the fact that the local committee of the Board had not, at the relevant time, been approved by the Home Secretary – the Board lost the case, and in addition had to pay costs. Clearly, this bungling on the part of the Board was not terribly impressive.

Nevertheless, the *Daily Miror* was cheerful about the outcome: 'It is now evident that the Race Relations Act has teeth – that it can and will be made to bite.'[6]

Side by side with its concern with racist behaviour, the Council was at least equally involved in campaigning over immigrant legislation. The British Nationality Act of 1948 created a single category of British subjects. This permitted a free flow of immigrants from the Commonwealth to Britain; indeed they were induced to come, in order to swell the depleted workforce after the war. The National Health Service and London Transport were amongst the largest concerns which wooed people from their own countries with promises of work – often jobs which the indigenous workers were reluctant to take. Once the country had got the people it wanted, it could afford to bow to racist pressures to restrict immigration, and this was engineered through the Commonwealth Immigrants Act 1962. The Act introduced a system of entry permits, and it was designed in such a way that black members of the Commonwealth were affected by the rules rather than whites. The Council complained that there was no right of appeal against the decision of an immigration officer at the port of entry; also, that the offence of 'harbouring' illegal immigrants would worsen accommodation problems for all black people in Britain.

Far worse, however, was the Commonwealth Immigrants Act of 1968; Patricia Hewitt quite properly calls it a 'shameful betrayal'.[7] There were thousands of people of Asian origin living in East Africa who, on the independence of the country in which they lived, had elected to remain as UK citizens rather than take up the citizenship of the new nation. They did so in the full understanding that they retained the right of entry to Britain, should they for any reason – such as harassment from the government of the former colony – wish to exercise it. The new Act effectively abolished this automatic right of entry and substituted a quota system; the effect was that only a tiny fraction of those wanting to emigrate were allowed to do so. Applicants waited, sometimes for years, before their applica-

tions were processed. The investigations and interviews conducted through the various British High Commissions to check
on the authenticity of the identities and *bona fides* of the
applicants were all too often callous, conducted in an atmosphere of hostile mistrust, and above all, they took months and
months. Asians desperate enough to leave Africa before they
had their papers in order found themselves the victims of the
'shuttlecock', whereby airlines flew families from country to
country in the face of Britain's refusal to accept them. Roy
Hattersley recently admitted that the 1968 Act was a 'mistake';
other people at the time had rather stronger things to say about
it. The International Commission of Jurists, for example,
claimed that it had removed Britain's claim to be a bastion of
civil liberties.

In 1970, the Conservatives took over from Labour, and in
1971 they passed their own Immigration Act, based on the
concept of 'patriality', with a complicated entry scheme and a
plethora of citizen categories. Its provisions – such as that those
with one grandparent born in Britain would be allowed to enter
the country to seek work – were clearly designed to favour the
whites of the 'Old' Commonwealth. Before it passed into law,
the Council warned of its consequences: 'The Immigration Bill
poses one of the worst threats to civil liberty for a long time. It
will condemn racial minorities to permanent insecurity. It will
divide the nation and the Commonwealth into patrials and
non-patrials – belongers and non-belongers.'[8] The story of the
three Acts (of 1962, 1968 and 1971) illustrates how both the
major political parties of the time were quite ready to appease
popular racist sentiment in order to curry favour with the
basest elements of the electorate.

During 1981, the Council combined with AGIN (Action
Group on Immigration and Nationality) to oppose what
became of the British Nationality Act. The Act introduced a
three-tier structure: full British citizenship; citizenship of
dependent territories; and 'overseas' British citizenship for the
rest. The effect of the tripartite division is to condemn nearly a
quarter of a million people to third-class status with no rights at

all. In addition, the Act perpetuates the right of the Home Secretary to reject an application for naturalisation on the basis of secret police reports, with no requirement that reasons be given. In 1982, on AGIN's behalf, the Council published a practical guide to the Act designed to help people cope with its complexities.

THE RIGHTS OF CHILDREN

In 1967, the Cobden Trust[9] published Nan Berger's *The Rights of Children and Young Persons*. Comprehensive coverage of the whole gamut of issues (which included juvenile courts, legal disabilities, handicap, nationality, paid employment, and illegitimacy) provided distressing evidence for the view that children were more or less at the mercy of adult discretion. Amongst all these issues, two in particular were given special attention by the NCCL, and it is on these that I wish to dwell in this section. They are religion in schools and corporal punishment.

One of the grossest impositions on school children, then as now, is religious indoctrination. Under the terms of the 1944 Education Act, every school day has to start with an act of collective worship, and in addition, religious instruction is the only subject (not excluding English and Maths) which the law requires to be taught in school. Although there are provisions to allow individual teachers and pupils (the latter, only on parental request) to absent themselves from the act of worship, the inevitable embarrassment (especially for children) of withdrawing conspicuously in this way, is great. Consequently, many attend who would prefer not to.

If we wish to have an educational system based on the spirit of intellectual enquiry, then this will be subverted if we found the whole school ethic on 'received' wisdom, from whatever religion. The essence of religious faith is that that which is believed is incapable of intellectual proof – if this were not so, disbelief would merely be a foolish rejection of the facts. The essence of education, on the other hand, involves the instilling of scepticism. These two concepts cannot be successfully married. Secondly, as the percentage of regular churchgoers amongst the population is about 15 per cent, it is against the principles of natural justice that Christianity should receive such spectacular state favouritism. Thirdly, even if a majority of the population were full Christians, it would still be an infringement of civil liberties to proceed with the present arrangements. Berger asked whether children should be 'indoctrinated with a religious faith (in schools which are paid for out of rates and taxes) at an age where they have no intellectual equipment to understand the implication of such indoctrination and can therefore not exercise any judgement'.[10] Fourthly, society is less and less homogeneous; it is increasingly multi-cultural, multi-racial and ethically diverse. The continued institutionalising of just one religion denies that diversity and accounts for the charges of racism levelled against the current effects of the 1944 Act. These views were reasserted at the Council's AGM in 1982, when a motion calling for the disestablishment of the Church of England, the abolition of the episcopal seats in the House of Lords, and an end to the religious provisions of the 1944 Act, was passed.

The corporal punishment of children in schools was opposed by NCCL in the strongest terms. In its pamphlet, 'Children Have Rights, Number One', such punishment is described as obsolete and 'should be abolished by law as it has been in most other comparable Western countries. At best it affords a lazy way out which avoids rather than solves behaviour problems. At worst, in the case of disturbed or deprived children, it can do real harm'.[11] In 1972, the Council launched a joint campaign with the Society of Teachers Opposed to Physical Punishment (STOPP); a member of the Council's executive drafted 'The Protection of Minors Bill' which was introduced by Baroness

Wootton of Abinger in the House of Lords at the end of 1974. The Bill, which sought to make corporal punishment illegal in schools, failed to get a second reading by a narrow majority.

In her study, Berger quotes one of the findings of the education inspectorate in 1963, in London, to the effect that violence was self-perpetuating: 'There is no doubt that the employment of harsh methods by teachers must tend towards the adoption of harsh standards by pupils when they leave school; it is in fact common knowledge that advocates of tough measures frequently put forward their own childhood treatment as a reason for continuing such methods in the next generation.'[12] She also makes it clear that there was little evidence to support the view that this sort of chastisement served its principal purpose; namely, preventing a repetition of the offence for which the punishment was awarded.

Of course the most controversial examples of corporal punishment were the birchings in the Isle of Man. Here, much of the emphasis of the campaign was on the degrading nature of the punishment for its recipient. I have never been able to feel that this is the central issue. Anyone who has any familiarity with conditions in penal institutions will accept at once that birching is not as degrading as imprisonment or detention. The real objection is not that the convicted boy (girls are not birched) is degraded, but that the whole system of justice is, on these occasions, most clearly contemptible. If society's response to offenders is at the best of times cruelly maladroit, in its recourse to birching it effectively abandons any pretence to the higher aspirations of penal theory. Here, quite simply, is malice and retribution.

The Council published Angela Kneale's *Against Birching* in 1973. The book stresses that the idea that violent crime should be met with violent punishment is not only erroneous but irrelevant, because the vast majority of birchings were administered for non-violent offences. One of the most ardent supporters of birching was an island magistrate called W. E. Quayle, who during the 1950s and 60s ordered birchings with depressing frequency. Quayle appeared on a Granada television programme in February 1961, and made the statement that 'There are many people who do not seem to realise that birching can only be imposed for serious offences such as crimes of violence.'[13] Kneale knew better, as she had researched the judicial use of birching with great thoroughness. Her comment on this remark by Quayle was: 'In the preceding year . . . Mr Quayle had ordered corporal punishment for two 10-year-old boys who stole foodstuffs from a snack bar, for two 13-year-olds for stealing a bicycle, for two London boys for house-breakings and thefts and for a 14-year-old Londoner for "demanding money with menaces".'[14]

In October 1975, the European Commission found against the United Kingdom in a case brought by NCCL, acting as solicitors for a young man who had been birched. NCCL argued that the practice breached both article 3 of the European Convention on Human Rights (which bans torture and inhuman or degrading treatment) and article 14 (which bans discrimination on the grounds of sex – only young men are ever birched).

This finding was met with considerable hostility from the islanders, who regard their judicial procedures as a domestic matter. But since the United Kingdom had signed the Human Rights Convention on behalf of the Isle of Man (for whose foreign affairs it is responsible), the islanders could not put their heads in the sand, despite suggestions from some members of the Tynwald that they should secede from the UK.

Although the island retains the power to birch on its statute books, no birchings have in fact taken place since 1975.

TRAVELLERS

The chief bane of the traveller's life, until its abolition in 1980, was Section 127 of the Highways Act 1959. This made it an offence to camp on the highway (which includes verges, however wide) and is particularly invidious because it expressly refers to gypsies, thus exempting 'respectable' groups such as holidaymakers: 'If without lawful authority or excuse . . . a hawker or other itinerant trader or a gypsy pitches a booth, stall or stand, or encamps, on a highway, he shall be guilty of an offence.' The official harassment constantly used against travellers is well illustrated in the case of the Lee family:

Joe Lee, his wife Mary and their three grown-up sons belong to the London area. In 1965 they parked within a mile of the Houses of Parliament at Lambeth. A series of forced removals sent them through Wandsworth and Tower Hamlets to Barking. Last year [1966] they tried stopping on the desolate Ministry of Defence airfield at Hornchurch, but were driven off by Havering Council. They pulled onto a cleared bomb site in West Ham. Their married daughter was waiting to have her baby baptised. Newham security patrol, with a police dog, came to move them. Mary and her daughter, baby Aaron in her arms, sat in the path of the towing lorry. Council men and police refused to move her. Prosecution followed and Joe tried to get onto a caravan site at Romford; but the site is being run down, and is scheduled for closure by 31 December 1967. With other families Joe stationed his caravan on adjacent land. All were summonsed for causing annoyance, but the case was dismissed. Without warning, on 27 January a party of men hired by Havering Council – because regular employees, members of the National Union of Public Employees, had declined the work – accompanied by 40 police, approached the caravans. Joe, his wife and sons and their neighbours sat on the drawbar of the first caravan and across a ladder on the ground. They tied themselves together with rope and refused to move, calling upon the young council-hired men to leave them alone. The men hesitated and the police began to drag men and women from their passive position. During an hour-long struggle a young social worker was thrown to the ground and taken to hospital with a bruised kidney. Three men were arrested for obstruction and threatening behaviour.

Joe and his family packed up once more and went back to the disused Hornchurch airfield. There he and forty other families faced eviction again, by Ministry of Defence land agents.[15]

The nature of this constant 'moving-on' procedure was altered by the decision in the George Bignall case. Some travellers were evicted from a refuse tip in the Borough of Bromley, and their caravans towed onto a bypass. They were then successfully prosecuted for encamping on the highway. However, NCCL advised one of them, Bignall, to test this decision in a higher court. The defence made two telling points. The first was the obvious one that as they had been towed onto the verge by the authorities, it could hardly be said that they had encamped there themselves. The second was a technical quibble. Bignall had been dealt with under Section 127 as a gypsy, but what was a gypsy? The 1959 Act remained silent on this, and the defence therefore argued that the next obvious and authoritative place to look was a dictionary. A dictionary was then produced describing gypsies as members of a tribe of Indian origin calling themselves Romany. But, it was argued, the prosecution in the court of first hearing had made no attempt to establish whether Bignall fitted this description. The appeal was allowed.

The importance of the decision was, of course, that it was no longer possible for local authorities to tow away travellers' caravans with impunity. Not only was this an unsatisfactory way of enforcing the law, but it actually rebounded on the authority. When Sevenoaks Council towed away two caravans from a site at Edenbridge, the police informed the Council that as a result of the Bignall case, it would itself be liable for the obstruction offence.

With Section 127 reduced in usefulness, the local authorities had no trouble finding other legal devices for harassing the gypsies. For example, Bromley (again) tried to remove a group of sixteen families from some building land by relying on Section 35 of the Orpington District Council Act 1954, which allowed action to be taken where the amenities of a particular area were affected. At Romford, the legal pretext used in the attempt to dislodge the gypsies was that they had caused a nuisance to a resident. Another method of deterring encampments was actually to build obstructions; mounds of rubble were dumped, trenches were dug. At the beginning of 1968, Bromley was said to be spending £4000 on site-blocking, and Walsall fully £10 000.

The breakthrough came in 1968 when Eric Lubbock MP (he of the 'Liberal Revival' at Orpington, and Chairperson of the Parliamentary Civil Liberties Group) successfully guided through its various Parliamentary stages what became the Caravan Sites Act. The chief principle which the Act established was that local councils would now have a legal duty to provide suitable sites for travellers. Whilst welcoming the new legislation, NCCL was seriously worried about two points in particular: first, that implementation of the new law as it related to the provision of sites (Part 2 of the Act) was not to be immediate, but at the discretion of the government; secondly, it was alarmed at the whole 'designation' procedure. As it turned out, both these issues became closely related and both gave as much trouble, and caused as much injustice, as the Council prophesied that they would.

The designation procedure was intended to work as follows: local authorities would make the provision for travellers as required in the legislation, a provision whose extent had to be measured against the number of gypsies in each area. Once they had satisfied central government that this provision was satisfactory and sufficient – or, in the alternative, once they had successfully applied for exemption, owing to reasons such as lack of land – then their areas could be designated. This meant that the authority could then refuse to cater for additional gypsies and could, indeed, prosecute them.

Because full implementation of the Act was delayed, the

Ministry of Housing issued a circular in 1968, emphasising the special difficulties which travellers experience in the winter months, and urging that temporary facilities be provided before the more permanent amenities required by the Act had had time to be established. The circular also strongly urged restraint in 'moving-on': 'The Ministers have repeatedly emphasized that gypsies should not be needlessly moved on from place to place until sites have been provided for them. It is particularly important that local authorities should not drive gypsies out of their areas, to become the responsibility of neighbouring authorities, in the period before a countrywide network of sites is established.'[16]

The worst fear of the Ministry, and of NCCL, was realised. There was a mad scramble to evict and prosecute, so that when eventually the Act was implemented, as many travellers as possible would have been pushed off into other areas. Evictions were enforced in Manchester, Dingwall in Scotland, Salford, Birmingham, and the London Borough of Hillingdon during 1969. Part 2 of the Act (the designation procedure) was finally implemented on 1 April 1970, but even after this very many authorities failed to take the Act seriously: some were slow to fulfil their obligations, some did so only partially and inadequately, and Walsall simply refused to comply with the law at all. When NCCL learnt from Lord Sandford of the Department of the Environment that no great efforts would be made by central government to force Walsall to come into line, its legal fund provided money for a Walsall gypsy to obtain counsel's opinion over the possibility of bringing an action against the authority. On 2 November 1971, Walsall's town clerk announced that the council had changed its mind and would be obeying the law after all. In 1984, some authorities have still not provided sites.

The 1968 Act had no effect in changing public bigotry. In October 1970, Sevenoaks Council was still digging protective trenches; at Bean, near Dartford, the local authority had drawn up rules for the caravan site so at odds with the gypsy way of life that it hoped by this means either to deter gypsies from using the site, or to be in a position to evict them for rule infringements; and the press continued to whip up hostility, with papers like Birmingham's *Sunday Mercury* accusing 'tinkers' of 'contempt for the law . . . the vilest despoliation . . . terrorisation of innocent families . . . stealing and intimidation. . . . Tinkers are not a minority group of reluctant and downtrodden outcasts as the law assumes, but a determined band of roughs who have chosen the life of outlaws and show no desire for any other'.[17] In a policy statement on 8 May 1972, the Gypsy Council explained that the Act which had initially been seen as a safeguard against harassment from the authorities was no such thing; the harassment was being intensified.

The Gypsy Council, NCCL and Michael Meacher MP, joined forces in 1972 to fight the first batch of designation orders, relating to Plymouth, St Helens and Stoke. They pointed out that in spite of the government's promise not to designate areas until suitable and sufficient sites had been provided in the relevant districts, the designations were now going ahead with less than half the required caravan pitches being available. In an adjournment debate in the Commons on 9 August, Meacher warned the government that the designation orders could provoke a crisis in community relations. He told of grossly inadequate facilities at the sites, and suggested that if the authorities were given financial inducements they would be more eager to conform to the spirit of the legislation. He also asked that temporary facilities should be available for gypsies in transit, and that social workers and teachers be attached to sites. In the House of Lords, Eric Lubbock (now Lord Avebury) attempted to defeat the three designation orders in a debate on 14 November, but he found very little support.

At the end of 1972, four years after the passing of the Act, there were only 58 sites, providing a total of 824 caravan pitches. Local authorities were said to be working towards figures of 164 sites with 2469 pitches; but as it was estimated that there were about 4000 gypsy families making up a population of around 20 000, even these proposed figures were, in NCCL's view, 'totally inadequate to meet the human need'.[18]

RELUCTANT SERVICEMEN

My husband was a boy recruit in the Royal Navy. He is now 19 with 8 more long years of service looming up. He is being treated by the naval psychiatrist for depression and has been for some while now. Surely the answer would be, if his work and separation from home is making him depressed, he should be allowed to take another job of work outside the Navy. But of course the Navy do not see it in this light.

I realise that I am only one wife in many hundreds who want their husband to be husbands and fathers, instead of virtual strangers. After all, Britain is renowned as a free country. Who has the right to take twelve years of a boy's life away, which he may regret? A 15 year old boy doesn't know what life has to offer until perhaps it's too late and he is committed to serve in Her Majesty's Navy.[19]

In the late 1960s, NCCL was constantly receiving letters like this, either from relatives and wives, or from the servicemen themselves. Although there were several unfair procedures in service recruitment, the chief issue for the Council was the long contract signed by boys of 15 and 16. This was usually for 9 years, but, so far from being made more flexible by the fact that the recruit was under age, did not begin to apply until he reached 18. A 15-year-old, signing such a contract, was therefore binding himself for twelve years. Parental consent was required, but as in the case of the detention of a child under the Mental Deficiency Act 1913, such consent could not be withdrawn.

Furthermore, the consent procedure had a major loophole

working in favour of the military authorities, which came to light when a young soldier complained to NCCL that he had joined up without any parental permission. The Ministry of Defence replied that, under the Army Act 1955, claims about the invalidity or absence of parental consent had to be made within three months; once this period had elapsed, it was too late to obtain any redress.

The effects on the reluctant servicemen themselves of being forced to continue for years and years ahead, on the basis of an ill-conceived and ill-informed enthusiasm when they were 15, were predictable. There were bed-wettings, delinquency, suicide and even physical mutilation – one man chopped off his friend's finger with an axe at his request. NCCL's general secretary, Tony Smythe, described the situation as 'a terrible harvest of human misery'.[20] There were, too, rather unpredictable effects. In 1963 two young airmen, a few years after signing 12-year contracts, came to the view that the holding of nuclear weapons by the RAF was immoral. They wrote to *Peace News* asking that those interested in setting up a CND group in the RAF should get in touch with them. It was not a great surprise that they were then sentenced to four months' imprisonment under the Air Force Act, for conduct liable to be disruptive of discipline.

The first important case for NCCL was that of a Navy stoker called John Mayhew. He had enlisted in 1957 at the age of 16, and very quickly realised that he had made a mistake. One of the ways in which men could leave the services before the expiry of their contract time was by purchasing discharge; the difficulty was that the rules governing such discharges kept changing. At one point, a minimum of $4\frac{1}{2}$ years had to be served before a purchase discharge would be considered. As Mayhew saved up the money and steadily approached the qualifying date, the date itself receded as the government kept increasing the minimum period by 6 months. By 1966, when Mayhew first contacted the Council, the minimum period stood at 7 years. The hopelessness of his case had led Mayhew to desert for 14 months, for which he had been imprisoned for 42 days and then flown out to the Far East. Despite applying for discharge every 3 months, he was always refused.

Then, having successfully studied for some 'A' levels in the difficult surroundings of the stokers' mess, he was offered a place at the university of Bristol. Even his commanding officer was by this stage recommending that the Navy should let him go, but the Admiralty refused. On 3 August 1966, Nigel Fisher MP asked the Under-Secretary of State for the Royal Navy, Mr Mallalieu, in the House of Commons whether it were not the case that Mayhew would be better off as a willing student rather than an unwilling sailor. Mr Mallalieu's reply was that 'He will not miss his place at university.'[21] This was universally taken to mean that Mayhew would be discharged in time for the beginning of the academic term in October. However, in a Commons debate of 2 November, Mayhew not having been discharged, Joan Lestor renewed the attack on the Under-Secretary; his reply was that Mayhew would have to wait until some time in 1967. He was, finally, discharged in that year.

Discharge by purchase was not the only way out. Compassionate amd medical discharges were sometimes given. There were some unorthodox methods too: feigned (or real) homosexuality; standing as a Parliamentary candidate (since restricted to successful candidates); desertion; repeated absence without leave; and, reminding one rather of the Cairo Parliament brouhaha, left-wing political sympathies, as manifested, for example, in purchasing the *Morning Star* or tuning in to East European radio stations!

Another route to freedom was through the Conscientious Objector Advisory Tribunal. The Tribunal was charged with the task of identifying 'genuine' COs. The applications of Cossey and Blomfield for registration as COs, heard on 27 October 1969, illustrate some of the difficulties. Blomfield's argument was based on his opposition to the use of nuclear weapons, and the conduct of the war in Vietnam; he was not, that is to say, an absolute pacifist, and this 'selective pacifism' was attacked by the Tribunal. He experienced the same hostility to moral (as opposed to religious) arguments as did potential COs in the war. On the other hand, it was precisely because Cossey's objection was religiously-based that it too ran into trouble. He had been baptised as an Anglican but had recently been attending Roman Catholic services; the Tribunal pointed out that as neither of these churches were doctrinally opposed to war, Cossey's argument was thereby weakened. In the event, Cossey succeeded in being discharged, but the nature of the arguments at the Tribunal underlined how unsatisfactorily subjective the whole system was.

In July 1967 the Latey Committee, which had been asked to review the whole position of boy entrants to the forces, presented its report, and on 5 February 1968, the Minister of Defence for Administration, Gerry Reynolds, announced what action he intended to take in the light of it. The initial period of three months during which boys were allowed to buy themselves out for £20 was to be extended to six months; parental consent would be required for all entrants up to 18 (instead of $17\frac{1}{2}$); and potential COs would no longer have to serve ninety days in detention before being allowed to appear before a Tribunal. However, to the Committee's crucial proposal that all boy entrants should be able to obtain a discharge three months after their eighteenth birthday, Reynolds gave a resounding 'no'. Whilst welcoming the minor improvements, the Council felt that it had been cheated of the main prize, and decided to redouble its efforts. It was not just that the existing scheme was inhumane, but that young men were being deprived of statutory rights which they would have enjoyed as civilians, under the Infants Relief Act of 1874 (which provides protection for 'infants' – those under the age of majority – who enter into contracts to their gross disadvantage).

NCCL seemed to derive some comfort from the fact that, whilst 'holding the line', Reynolds admitted in public more than once that the long contract system was morally indefensible, and could only be justified because of the nation's security needs. The Council decided to explore the possibility of an international remedy, and submitted four cases to the European Commission on Human Rights. The claim was based on three articles in the Human Rights Convention: first, that no one shall be held in servitude (article 4 (i)); secondly, that citizens are entitled to a fair judicial hearing before an independent tribunal within a reasonable time (article 6); and thirdly, that citizens shall have an effective remedy before a national authority (article 13). Unfortunately, the application was held to be inadmissible.

Meanwhile the files were swelling all the time at the Council's offices, often with stories of great personal distress. Here is an extract from one letter received:

I was beginning to think that perhaps nobody in the 'outside world' is interested in our problem. Your Council provides a relief for me because if I don't inform somebody of my predicament I'm afraid I will be on the verge of a breakdown. I am very near to it now incidentally. I joined the Royal Navy in 1964 . . . and I have done nothing but the work of a mediaeval servant. The reason why I have stayed in up to now is because of my father's behalf. He was terribly proud of his only son joining up in the RN. I have never really liked the life, and the past 18 months have just gone from bad to worse. So acute is my depression that I recently went on a long week-end to my home with the full intention of not returning to the ship. On the night I was supposed to return I was that depressed with my life that I felt that I just could not go on living so I picked up a razor blade and slashed my wrists. . . . After seeing a civilian psychiatrist and spending a week in hospital a medical escort came to collect me and take me to ————. I am now back on board. I am still in a state of deep depression and I am afraid that if I am not released from the RN soon I will desert. In the civilian hospital I was treated like a human being, but when I arrived at ———— I was treated as an animal. The RN psychiatrist treated me as a silly boy who would grow out of this passing phase. The 'doctor' on board treated me for depression and my interview with him lasted no more than 3 minutes. . . . Surely this is not the state for an 18 year old to be in. I have been denied all the rights of a young person in civil life. All I want is to be a normal person, as I would be in 'civvy street'.[22]

In March, 1969, the Council wrote a report called *Civil Liberties and Service Recruitment* which included details of 75 individual cases. It was sent to teachers and employment agencies in the hope that the message would penetrate to the young that signing long contracts could be disastrous. At the same time, Eric Lubbock MP, who chaired the Parliamentary Civil Liberties group, put down an early day motion welcoming the assurances that had been given on behalf of the Ministry of Defence by Dr David Owen, to the effect that the government was still considering the possibility of implementing the Latey recommendation about automatic discharge three months after the recruit's eighteenth birthday.

Once Roy Hattersley had taken over from Reynolds, things began to move slightly more quickly. Hattersley announced in November 1969 that a committee (chaired by Lord Donaldson) would be established to look at the question again. Several MPs, including Frank Allaun and Nigel Fisher, wanted NCCL's general secretary, Tony Smythe, on the committee, but Hattersley insisted on having people as yet uncommitted to a strong view. In the same month he was telling an NCCL deputation that, like Reynolds, he found the long contract system 'morally distasteful'[23] but that defence commitments left the government little alternative. However, once the Donaldson Committee had reported, the new Conservative government accepted most of its proposals. On the crucial point of automatic right of discharge at eighteen, the government compromised. They would allow men to elect to leave the service at that age, but they would have to wait a further 3 years, until they were 21, before actually being discharged. This was harsh, but obviously better than being stuck with another 6- or 7-years' service.

It was a minor victory; many of the Council's other proposals sent to the Committee – the appointment of a military ombudsman, and the right of servicemen to join trade unions – were ignored. Despite the disappointment at the outcome, the official callousness had been replaced by caution, the claims of personal freedom were allowed at least some sway alongside the exigencies of the nation's defence, and just a little more unhappiness had been mitigated or prevented. It all counts.

NORTHERN IRELAND

It was not that successive governments had not been warned. As decade followed decade for 40 years or more, the signals had not so much been given as thrust before the faces of the politicians. Long ago, in 1936, the NCCL had set up a Commission of Enquiry to examine the entrails of the 'Ulster Crisis' and had made a prognosis not so very different from the one made by our Conference on Northern Ireland in September 1969. The trouble was, they simply never listened. Or if they listened, they didn't hear. Or if they heard, they continued to sit on their hands.

Perhaps it is the way of politics, but tell that to the children who saw their homes burn and whose lungs were filled with CS Gas. Tell it to the idle men, the frightened women, the homeless families of Londonderry and Belfast. Tell it, rather, to the Marines and the military who had to be brought in to keep the Catholic poor from the Protestant poor and the 'B' Specials from them both (*NCCL Annual Report*, 1970).

The seventies opened in dismal fashion. The enthusiasm generated by the Civil Rights Movement, which brought hope of long-awaited reform, had dissipated amidst sectarian murders, patrolling British troops and the birth of the Provisionals. Over 2000 people died from terrorist violence, and over 22 000 were injured. The decade witnessed security operations dependent upon British Army presence; internment; 'Bloody Sunday'; Direct Rule and the collapse of the power sharing Executive; suspension of jury trial; the bombing campaign in Britain; the Prevention of Terrorism Act and deaths of school children from plastic bullets.

When Northern Ireland's boundaries were drawn in 1922, they gave the Unionists a comfortable two to one majority. But from the start, the Protestant majority felt deeply insecure, distrusting both Britain as inherently unreliable and the 26 counties to the South as a base for Republican agitation.

The Stormont Parliament, permanently dominated by the Ulster Unionist majority, reflected this insecurity. In local Government, in areas where Catholics were in a majority, electoral boundaries were manipulated to guarantee Unionist domination. Discrimination and segregation in employment prevailed. Protestant areas were financed and developed in preference to predominantly Catholic ones. Segregated schooling sharpened religious divisions and facilitated overt and covert discrimination.

But protection of the entity of Northern Ireland was considered paramount. 'Temporary' legislation was introduced giving Stormont and the police (which were overwhelmingly Protestant) powers which were the envy of the South African Minister of Justice. The Special Powers Acts, introduced first in 1922 and made permanent in 1933, gave security forces the power to arrest without warrant, detain without trial, to enter and search homes without warrant, to impose a curfew, to prohibit meetings, assemblies and processions, the power to hang and the power to whip.

In 1934, the newly formed National Council for Civil Liberties turned its eyes to events in the province. The prospect of permanent legislation prompted it to set up an independent commission of enquiry. The commission was a distinguished one. Its secretary, Neil Lawson, was a young barrister at the time and later became a Court of Appeal Judge.

The report was published in 1936. Its conclusions were damning and are still relevant today:

First, that through the operation of the Special Powers Acts contempt has been begotten for the representative institutions of Government.

Secondly, that through the use of Special Powers individual liberty is no longer protected by law, but is at the arbitrary disposition of the Executive. This abrogation of the rule of law has been so practised as to bring the freedom of the subject into contempt.

Thirdly, that the Northern Irish Government has used Special Powers towards securing the domination of one particular political faction and, at the same time, towards curtailing the lawful activities of its opponents. The driving of legitimate movement underground into illegality, the intimidating or branding as law breakers of their adherents, however innocent of crime, has tended to encourage violence and bigotry on the part of the Government's supporters as well as to beget in its opponents an intolerance of the 'law and order' thus maintained. The Government's policy is thus driving its opponents into the ways of extremists.[24]

The 1936 Report was prophetic and became the cornerstone of the NCCL's involvement in Northern Ireland.

As the situation deteriorated, so NCCL's involvement increased. In 1959, the Council called for a full enquiry into the 'continued violation of civil liberties in Northern Ireland'. In 1962, the executive committee produced a seven-point plan for Northern Ireland civil liberties, including repeal of the Special Powers Acts, and boundary and electoral reforms.

An NCCL Conference on Northern Ireland in 1965 brought together for the first time representatives of all political parties in Northern Ireland, the trade unions, other pressure groups, and civil rights' organisations. It called for a Royal Commission to examine the constitutional foundation of Northern Ireland, the Government of Ireland Act 1920. This gave an assurance that Northern Ireland would be governed on the basis of religious equality for its inhabitants.

The civil rights' movement which mushroomed in the late

1960s was basically seeking the fulfilment of this guarantee. It began by trying to use the law, but in 1966 the movement was refused legal aid to finance a test case on housing discrimination, and concluded that pursuing legal redress was fruitless. Two years later, the ban on Republican Clubs under the Special Powers Act was challenged in court, but the case was finally lost in the House of Lords, in June 1969. Outside the courtroom, the Northern Ireland Civil Rights Association (NICRA), established with NCCL help in 1967, concentrated on mass campaigning and publicity as the most effective means of change.

By 1968 the civil rights' movement had begun to organise marches and rallies. These were attacked by Protestant extremists. The police did nothing to protect the marchers, and indeed added their own hostility and aggression. In October 1968, a march in Londonderry was banned on the grounds that it clashed with an Apprentice Boys' march. (This was later found to have been invented for the occasion.) The march went ahead anyway and was violently attacked by the police.

In January 1969, the 'B' Specials ambushed a march from Belfast to Londonderry, organised by People's Democracy. In August, police did not intervene when a number of Catholic areas in Belfast were burnt. Later that month the British Army was brought in to take over from the police. A package of reforms was pushed through under pressure from Westminster. But NCCL condemned these as belated and insufficient. The reconstituted Royal Ulster Constabulary and the British Army failed to allay the fears of the inhabitants of Catholic enclaves. Neither were demands for reform met.

Indeed the Army, untrained for police work, conducted extensive searches in Catholic areas. In July 1970, it imposed an illegal curfew in the Lower Falls area of Belfast in order to perform a house-to-house search. This led to violence between the soldiers and the community.

As the Army became not the protector of the minority community but the inheritor of the Unionists' Special Powers Acts, so the Provisional IRA was conceived, a split from the

'Official' Republican movement which continued its emphasis on political reform. In 1970, the first person died at the hands of the Army; in February 1971, the first soldier at the hands of the Provisionals.

In July 1971, the Army shot dead Seamus Cusack and William Beatty in Londonderry. An independent enquiry was refused and the main opposition group, the Social Democratic and Labour Party, withdrew from Stormont. NCCL visits to Northern Ireland by Tony Smythe and executive members became more frequent and their reports increasingly anxious. A detailed open letter from Tony Smythe to the Prime Minister set out 15 points, ranging from a condemnation of the Special Powers Acts to an urging of the adoption of a Bill of Rights. But it was largely ignored.

In August 1971, internment was re-introduced. The first internees were all Catholic. Detention without trial marked the abandonment of any pretence at upholding the rule of law. Twelve detainees were brutally ill-treated by being hooded, continually subjected to electronic noise, spread-eagled against a wall for up to 43 hours, deprived of sleep, and beaten. These actions were subsequently condemned by the European Human Rights Commission as torture. Two members of the Compton Commission, established by the British Government to investigate the allegations, upheld the use of these interrogation techniques, although a third, Lord Gardiner, condemned them as illegal and not morally justifiable.

A *Sunday Times* opinion poll carried out in November that year, found that British public opinion thought the Government had done a good job in Northern Ireland, that interrogation methods were right, the Compton Report fair and that internment would make things better.

The NCCL did what it could. The findings of the General Secretary's visits were incorporated into a broadsheet, *Speak Out*, which was sent to members in January 1972.

It was over 3 years before the authorities publicly admitted that internment had been a mistake. One case is typical of several pursued by NCCL at this time. Sean McGuigan was arrested in November 1971 and held for almost a year before being acquitted of most of the charges against him. The remaining charges were dropped. He was immediately arrested and interned, then released a second time having been in detention 14 months in all.

On 30 January 1972, a civil rights' march was organised in Londonderry. Since it contravened a Government ban, the organisers assumed that the Army would at some point block its progress. This duly happened, and the main march, between ten and twenty thousand strong, detoured to hold a meeting at Free Derry Corner. A crowd of a few hundred remained in front of the Army barricades. Stones and bottles were thrown. The Army replied with rubber bullets, CS gas and a water cannon spraying coloured dye.

Then at about 9.15 pm, soldiers of the Parachute Regiment deployed out from behind the barricades, on foot and in armoured cars. Shots were fired at the troops, and they also fired, although the question of who began the shooting was never established. At all events, the soldiers shot indiscriminately, while panic stricken members of the crowd tried to escape. Thirteen people were killed and another thirteen were seriously wounded. January 30 became known as 'Bloody Sunday'.

NCCL observers had been sent to Londonderry, but in trying to reach the town, were stopped and searched five times and were twice detained 'under Special Powers'. Their journey by road from the airport took eight and a half hours and their final release from a Londonderry RUC station occurred at 6 pm, *after* the shootings. Nevertheless, on-the-spot investigations were started that same evening. Later that week, two further representatives were sent to coordinate and record evidence from eye-witnesses. Some 600 statements were collected by the Derry Civil Rights Association and other community groups. When the government set up an inquiry by Lord Widgery into the events of that day, these reports were, with the consent of those involved, made available. The same evidence was passed to Professor Sam Dash of the International League for the Rights of Man, who, working from the same material as Lord Widgery, reached different conclusions and confirmed NCCL's deep concern at the inadequacy of the Widgery Report. These were contained in an NCCL publication published in June that year entitled *Justice Denied: a Challenge to Lord Widgery's Report on Bloody Sunday*. The essential difference was that Widgery saw the army's errors, but gave individuals the benefit of the doubt; Dash's view was that the security forces had been criminally reckless.

One further consequence of 'Bloody Sunday' was the decision by the British Government to prorogue the Stormont Parliament and impose direct rule from Westminster. With this came an attempt to 'normalise the crisis'. William Whitelaw, the new Northern Ireland Secretary, immediately released over seventy internees and promised personally to review the cases of the remaining 728. The Special Powers Acts were examined by Lord Diplock with a view to repeal.

But the process of 'normalisation', of dealing with suspected terrorists through the criminal courts, produced its own sequel of human rights' violations. The Emergency Provisions Act, which replaced the Special Powers Acts in 1973, abolished jury trial for 'scheduled offices' (those thought likely to relate to terrorism), reversed the burden of proof on bail applications, and admitted hearsay and 'confession' statements as evidence (unless the defendant could prove these were obtained improperly).

Patricia Hewitt, as NCCL's General Secretary, consistently argued for the Act's repeal. The allegation of sectarian bias among Northern Ireland juries – the reason given for their abolition – was never substantiated. More important, the two communities in Northern Ireland had effectively been policed under different systems since 1970; the Protestant Community by the largely Protestant RUC, which was able to bring suspects to court; and the Catholic areas, which were policed by the Army, with suspects ending up only too often in internment.

The absence of juries remains a major factor in the lack of confidence in the special courts. This was revealed in research undertaken by the Cobden Trust and published in 1973 in *Justice in Northern Ireland: a Study in Social Confidence*. A public opinion survey carried out in 1980 showed that a majority within both communities favoured the restoration of jury trial. The most recent Cobden research published in 1983, based on court surveys, suggests that up to 40 per cent of cases which come before the non-jury courts have no recognisable 'terrorist' connection.[25]

The Emergency Provisions Act also authorised the detention of suspects for up to 72 hours. As confession statements were now *prima facie* admissible, this encouraged the police to use the extended detention periods to obtain the necessary 'confession'.

In 1977, two special RUC interrogation centres were opened at Castlereagh and Armagh. Police doctors themselves became concerned at what they saw, but their representations were ignored. In 1978, following an Amnesty International investigation which concluded that complaints of ill-treatment were well founded, the Government established yet another Committee of Enquiry, this time under Judge Bennett. That enquiry found beyond doubt that suspects in RUC custody had been injured, and that the injuries were not 'self-inflicted' as suggested by the authorities. A series of recommendations ensued. Dermot Walsh's Cobden Trust study, referred to above, shows that RUC interrogation practices are still giving cause for concern and that the Bennett recommendations have not been fully implemented. Nor, the research concludes, were the post-Bennett procedures entirely effective in protecting the suspect in custody.

In the past 10 years, NCCL has argued that a lack of public confidence in the impartiality of the courts and judiciary strongly influence opponents of British rule in their decision to join the ranks of the para-militaries. Paradoxically, young idealists, aspiring to a higher standard of justice and a quality of life signally lacking in Northern Ireland, become active in outlawed organisations and thereby provide the rationale for the continued suspension of acceptable judicial standards.

The failure of the British army to contain the IRA and the recent success of Sinn Fein at the polls are the fruits of inadequate Government action – but not the only ones. In 1972, a bomb exploded in the officers' mess at Aldershot Barracks. One month later over 60 houses of Irish Republicans and civil rights activists in Britain were raided and address books, diaries, notebooks and leaflets were removed, together with their owners.

The intensive police watch on the Irish in Britain had begun. The following year, after two bomb explosions in London, the police carried out a series of raids on Irish immigrants. In November 1973, *Civil Liberty* warned: 'As the raids go on, the danger is that they will become an accepted part of police procedure along with detention and questioning without arrest. The police will have succeeded in infringing civil liberties by use of methods which have no value as a means of detection of crime, but only as a means of building up information and intelligence on radical groups not involved in any criminal activities.'[26] This brought a sharp rejoinder at the time from Robert Carr, then Home Secretary. He said the police would use whatever methods were necessary to apprehend the culprits.

In 1975, Kenneth Lennon was found dead in a ditch in Surrey. Forty-eight hours earlier he had spent 6 hours giving a statement to NCCL's Legal Officer, Larry Grant. He said he had been blackmailed into informing by Special Branch officers. Yet the 3 men convicted on his information had their appeal turned down.

That same year, 14 people were charged under the 1934 Incitement to Disaffection Act for possessing leaflets advising soldiers how to leave the Army if they wished to avoid service in Northern Ireland. NCCL solicitors were among the defence team, and the campaign around the case echoed the original campaign against the Bill in 1934.

In 1974, the Prevention of Terrorism (Temporary Provisions) Act, described by the then Home Secretary, Roy Jenkins, as draconian and unprecedented in peacetime, was passed. It banned the IRA and made it illegal to belong to or support a banned organisation, even if this support involved no illegal action. The police were empowered to hold anyone suspected of terrorism (defined as 'the use of violence for political ends') for up to 48 hours and, with the Home Secretary's consent, a further 5 days. NCCL opposed this, as it effectively suspended *habeas corpus*.

In Northern Ireland these extensive detention powers were added to those of the Emergency Provisions Act, and were used by the RUC there when the police desired a particularly lengthy interrogation of a suspect. Under the 1984 Bill (the legislation has to be renewed annually), the police powers to arrest and detain are extended to those supected of involvement in 'international terrorism'. In addition, a system of exclusion is permitted, which allows the Secretary of State to exclude suspected terrorists from the UK altogether, or to exclude them from Britain to Northern Ireland and vice versa. People excluded are not charged with criminal offences, are not told of the evidence against them, and therefore cannot prepare a defence. They have no trial and no appeal except to make 'representations' to an 'adviser' appointed by the Government.

From the start, NCCL determined that the campaign against the Prevention of Terrorism Acts should be a major priority. It published two pamphlets on the Acts, provided detailed briefings for all Parliamentary stages of the Bills, and took cases under the Acts to the European Human Rights Commission.

Initially, NCCL stood alone against the Bill; in 1974 the MPs voting against it could be counted in single figures. But over the years its use has shown that NCCL's criticism was justified, and numerous organisations have joined the campaign against it. In 1983 the Labour Party, for the first time, opposed the revised Prevention of Terrorism Bill.

5 1975–84

PRISONS

From 31 August to 3 September 1976, prisoners occupied the maximum security wings at Hull, in protest at the treatment of another prisoner, Martin Clifford. Once the protest was over, prison officers began to victimise and assault those who had taken part. The prisoners' rights' organisation, PROP, held an unofficial enquiry. A committee of seven was formed, headed by a senior barrister, and evidence was taken from relatives, friends and ex-prisoners, as well as prisoners still in jail, and whose testimony was smuggled out written on lavatory paper. One account of the beatings read as follows: 'The screws split up into groups of about four or five and worked their way up and down the line of cells. It was systematic and co-ordinated – either they would charge into a cell, push the prisoner on to the floor and kick him into a corner . . . or they would drag you out with your arms and legs flailing and hurl you against a wall, landing blows to the head, back, legs and kidneys.'[1] In another account, a mother described the treatment received by her son: 'A few days later he was beaten up again and kicked between the legs; this dropped him to his knees and a pot of urine (not his own) was poured over him. He was not allowed to wash or change his clothing for days. He had no blankets and when he complained about being cold he was given a couple of blankets. On unfolding them he was sickened to find them smeared in human excrement. The food during this period was not fit to eat and everything was swimming in urine.'[2]

After the prisoners' demonstration, 180 inmates were

113

charged with disciplinary offences under the Prison Rules; as they were serious charges, they had to be dealt with by the Board of Visitors rather than the governor. These Boards sit in such cases as a judicial authority with extensive powers. The members are predominantly elderly white male establishment figures, at least half of them being magistrates. They are appointed by the Home Office and the method of selection is secret.

Now, although Prison Rule 49 (2) enjoins Boards in disciplinary hearings to give a prisoner 'a full opportunity of hearing what is alleged against him and of presenting his own case'; and although Form 1145 given to each accused, contains the following undertaking: 'If you want to call witnesses ask the Chairman for permission to do so. Tell him who they are and what you think their evidence will prove. If the Board think that the witnesses may be able to give useful evidence, they will hear them'; yet in spite of these official reassurances, the actual conduct of the Hull prisoners' hearings was very different. They were not allowed to call any defence witnesses. They were not allowed to be legally represented. And the individual hearings were, in many instances, extraordinarily brief. Peter Rajah, for example, faced 4 charges and his hearing took 15 minutes; then the Board retired for 1 minute 40 seconds. Rajah's 'award' was 390 days loss of remission, which is equivalent to an additional prison sentence of 19 months.

A small group of prisoners who had been dealt with thus summarily by the Board pursued their grievance in the courts, one of them being legally represented by NCCL. The Divisional Court found against them. Lord Widgery, the Lord Chief Justice, stated that it would be wrong for the courts to entertain legal actions by disgruntled prisoners. Governors' lives would thereby be rendered impossible, he argued. But the Court of Appeal found for the prisoners, establishing that Boards were obliged to act in accordance with the principles of natural justice. This having been established, it was directed that the case be returned to the Divisional Court for judgement; and eventually, in June 1979, almost three years after the actual disturbances, 17 out of the 25 charges against the six prisoners were quashed. This case, *R* v. *Board of Visitors of Hull Prison, ex parte St Germain*, was of key importance, as NCCL recognised: 'For the first time since the origins of the present prisons system in the nineteenth century a court of law was recognising that a person in prison may have rights and not just privileges.'[3]

The *Germain* decision was to be cited in the legal arguments over the notorious 'control unit', set up in Wakefield Prison in 1974. It was intended to contain prisoners who were thought to be especially disruptive. The regime in the unit was designed to cow inmates into acquiescence. There was an initial period of 90 days of solitary confinement, in which the prisoner was kept in the cell for 23 hours a day, with an hour for exercise. No association with other prisoners was allowed. If the prisoner 'cooperated', he then graduated to a second phase, also of 90 days' duration, during which some limited association was permitted. Only after the full 180 days had been satisfactorily completed would the inmate be returned to mainstream prison life. An especially inhumane feature of the system was that any misbehaviour by the prisoner meant that he would have to go back to day one and start the whole process again. The mental anxiety resulting from these arrangements ('all snakes, no ladders' in the words of one judge[4]) was at least as severe as that imposed on those awaiting parole decisions. NCCL brought together various prisoners' rights and penal reform groups to oppose the units, which fairly quickly were put out of use.

One prisoner, Michael Williams, who had served the full 180 days in the unit, brought an action against the Home Office; he claimed that he had suffered mentally as a result of being kept in the unit. The Council supported him and its legal officer, Harriet Harman (now the Labour MP for Peckham) took up the case. The main argument used by NCCL was that, as the Prison Rules limited solitary confinement to 56 days, the 90-day system in the unit was unlawful. In addition, *Germain* was cited.

The Williams decision, which the prisoner lost, dealt with both of these points. With regard to the Prison Rules, the judge stated that, although they had clearly been breached, they were regulatory rather than mandatory – in other words, like the Judges' Rules, they did not have the force of law and could not be enforced. Secondly, the judge decided that the rule in *Germain* did not apply in this case, as the unit was not a punishment but an administrative measure!

Another crucial test case for prisoners' rights, and one to which NCCL gave considerable publicity, was that of Sydney Golder, who was charged with taking part in a disturbance in Parkhurst Prison in 1969. As Golder suspected that this charge, which he denied, had contributed to his having been refused parole, he requested permission of the Secretary of State to consult a solicitor in order to initiate libel proceedings. The permission was required by Prison Rule 34 (8); it was refused. Golder took the case to the European Court of Human Rights at Strasbourg, relying on two articles in the Convention on Human Rights. Under article 6(1) 'everyone is entitled to a fair and public hearing within a reasonable time by an independent and impartial tribunal'. Golder argued that, by denying him access to legal advice, the Secretary of State was effectively denying him a fair hearing. The British Government argued that the right to a fair hearing did not mean that there was a right actually to have a hearing. The Court rejected the Government's argument and agreed with Golder.

Article 8 was also invoked by Golder. This guarantees the right of correspondence without interference by a public authority. The Government's line here was even more bizarre; it argued that, as Golder had stuck to Prison Rule 34(8) and not attempted to write to a solicitor, it could not be said that his correspondence had been interfered with. All twelve judges of the Court rejected this absurdity: 'Impeding someone from even initiating correspondence constitutes the most far-reaching form of interference.'[5] Golder had won his case, and the Court now required the British Government to conform to the Convention.

The manner in which the Home Office manoeuvred around the Court's decision was disgraceful. In 1975, the year of the

Court's decision, it issued a Circular Instruction, which insisted that 'no obstacles must be put in the way of inmates wishing to bring legal proceedings in any civil matter'. Prison Governors were instructed to afford facilities to prisoners so that they might seek legal advice, 'unless the case falls within sub-paragraph (ii) below'. This sub-paragraph explained that facilities 'are not to be granted until the inmate has ventilated his complaint through the normal existing internal channels, i.e. by petition to the Secretary of State OR by application to the Board of Visitors OR a visiting Officer of the Secretary of State OR under the procedures of CI 88/1961'.[6] It was, of course, precisely his dissatisfaction with the internal channels that had led Golder to take his complaint to Strasbourg. By insisting on the prisoner first using the internal complaints' procedure, the Home Office effectively neutered the Strasbourg decision, because the chief feature of the complaints' procedure was that cases could be delayed in bureaucratic red tape more or less indefinitely. According to Cohen and Taylor, the Circular 'really takes prisoners back to square one with a vengeance'.[7]

The Home Office's response to the Golder case should be seen not as an isolated example of callous duplicity, but of a piece with all its dealing with prisoners. The hallmarks of its policy are obsessive secrecy, and the creation of regulations so labyrinthine in their complexity that few inmates stand a chance of understanding them, let alone contesting them successfully. Prison life is regulated by instructions contained in the *Governors' Handbook*; a set of Standing Orders, and circular instructions amending and elaborating them; and the Prison Rules, a series of statutory instruments. Apart from the Prison Rules, all these documents are secret, and neither prisoners nor public can gain access to them. The disastrous effects of this hugger-mugger are well documented in Cohen and Taylor's *Prison Secrets*, jointly published by NCCL and Radical Alternatives to Prison, and referred to above.

One of the consequences of a secret system is habitual mendacity from those who operate it. A good example of this

occurred after the quelling of a protest in D-wing of Wormwood
Scrubs on 31 August 1979. A special squad of officers (badly)
trained in MUFTI (minimum use of force tactical intervention) stormed the wing and, after seven minutes, 60 prisoners
and 14 officers had been injured – the 'minimum' and the
'tactical' were less in evidence than the 'force'. Indeed, the
Home Office admitted that this special squad had not received
anything like proper training. The first official report stated
that no prisoners had been injured; this was later amended to
the effect that 5 prisoners had been admitted to hospital; the
final tally, about a month after the incident, was given as 53.
The official Home Office statement dealing with these contra-
dictions, acknowledged that they had been caught out in an
embarassing way: 'Incorrect statements were made and were
not subsequently corrected. This is wholly unacceptable both
as a matter of public accountability and management responsibility.'[8] The Home Office placed much of the blame on the
governor, Mr Honey, who was subsequently moved to Prison
Department headquarters.

The Home Office document also highlighted an issue to
which NCCL has repeatedly drawn attention; namely, the
anomalous position of Visitors. We have already seen (in the
Hull Prison case) that they exercise a disciplinary role; but
members of the Board are also expected to give an ear to
complaints and pursue them in appropriate quarters, and in
general to be solicitous for prisoners' welfare. It is almost
impossible to combine these contradictory functions satisfactorily; and the Wormwood Scrubs report made it clear that the
Board had become so closely identified with the management
and staff, that its critical faculties had been blunted.

A final point on the Scrubs incident. The Director of Public
Prosecutions declined to institute proceedings against any of
the prison officers concerned, on the grounds that, although
there was *prima facie* evidence that unlawful assaults had taken
place, difficulties of identification and the absence of corrobora-
tion meant that individual officers could not be identified as
responsible. The Home Office report also concluded that, as 'it

is not possible to assign responsibility for a disciplinary offence
to an individual officer',[9] no disciplinary proceedings could be
brought. In one sense, this attitude is understandable; nobody
wants to see the distress of prosecution visited on those against
whom there is insufficient evidence. On the other hand, it is
surely unsatisfactory that those who use unlawful violence *in
concert* should, because of that very fact, place themselves in a
less dangerous position as regards possible judicial reprisal
than the sole offender.

One feature of the prison system which NCCL has
repeatedly attacked is the Parole Board. At a cursory view, it
appears an excellent idea that those sentenced to a particular
term of years can, through its operation, be released early on
parole. However, there are serious objections. In the first place,
parole introduces a considerable degree of indeterminancy in
sentencing, and the effect of this is that prisoners experience
great mental anxiety in the period before their case is reviewed
by the Board. Secondly, the Board does not give reasons as to
why parole has been refused, and this also is a source of great
anxiety to the applicant. A third point is well explained by Bill
Birtles, a barrister and member of the Council's executive:
'Parole decisions tend, in practice, to be based on pre-sentence
characteristics (e.g. duration of criminal career, type of crime,
married/single) which criminological research has shown to be
the best predictors of recidivism. These pre-sentence characteristics often figure as aggravating or mitigating factors in the
trial judge's deliberations to determine sentence. Parole,
therefore, results in offenders with good pre-sentence characteristics being rewarded twice and offenders with bad pre-
sentence characteristics being penalised twice.'[10]

NCCL has also campaigned for the incorporation of the
prison medical service into the NHS; at the moment, the fact
that prison doctors are in a category of their own, separated
from their colleagues in the 'outside world', raises disturbing
questions about the consequences for the doctor-patient relationship. Under the present arrangements, the inmates see the
doctor as merely another part of the disciplinary establishment

– and especially because of the use of what is known colloquially as the 'liquid cosh'. In 1977, Dr Whitehead, writing in *Pulse*
on 15 October, stated that there was 'considerable evidence
that large numbers of prisoners are given psychotropic drugs,
not because they are suffering from serious mental illness, but
as a form of control'. In 1978, the *Sunday Times* printed a leaked
article from the then secret *Prison Medical Journal*. The article
described how 'psychopaths' had been given the drug depixol
with the result that 'discipline was considerably improved'.[11]
Although the prison authorities insist that such drugs are only
ever administered voluntarily, this is not always the case; for
example, a remand prisoner at Brixton called Paul Barbara,
who refused to take largactil, had it forcibly injected into his
buttocks.[12] George Ince, a Gartree prisoner, had no previous
history of mental illness but had slashed his wrists after being
placed in solitary confinement. Dr Whitehead, who examined
Ince in 1977, found that he had, at various times, been given
largactil, valium, depixol, chloral hydrate and mogadon, and
concluded that Ince 'has received treatment that should be
totally unacceptable in a civilised society'.[13]

The most persistent criticism of the prison system, of course,
is that it is so physically squalid as to be truly degrading for
both prisoners and staff. The overcrowding, the lack of proper
exercise, the inadequacy of educational provision – all these
combine with the pettifogging restrictions, the endless and
complicated bureaucracy of rules, to create a truly mindless
and mean-spirited world-in-miniature. You do not have to go
to the radical press for this message; even those on the political
right, wedded to concepts of retribution, admit that our prisons
do not succeed in protecting the public (because recidivism is
so high), are a liability to the tax-payer, and cannot hope to
rehabilitate or reform any who pass through their gates. Even
those who run the prisons no longer pretend. In a famous recent
incident, John McCarthy, as governor of Wormwood Scrubs,
wrote to *The Times* describing his prison as a penal dustbin.
Later that paper wrote in a leading article:

Mr Whitelaw knows that Mr McCarthy is right, yet he has capitulated to the arrogant and ignorant demands of the law and order lobby at the last Conservative conference. That is a pity, because it means the abandonment of a policy which would have resulted in less overcrowding in favour of one which has no predictable effect. It is not entirely Mr Whitelaw's fault. He inherited dangerously – inhumanly – overcrowded prisons, the fruits of many years of neglect by governments of both parties. The prisons particularly need the relief promised by the various forms of non-custodial help for offenders who should not be in prison at all but who are being sent there for want of alternatives. The fruits of that neglect are now being reaped, and something has to be done quickly to avert a catastrophe in our prisons.[14]

This is not *New Society* or *The Leveller*. When *The Times* starts to talk of inhuman conditions, and refers to prisoners who should not be incarcerated at all, even the most diehard reactionary is forced to concede the point: that the whole prison service is a disgraceful blot on a society which purports to be guided by principles of decency and fair play.

In the recent past, the Council has been receiving something like a thousand letters a year from prisoners, and has built up a specialised information and advice service for those areas in which many solicitors are unwilling or unable to operate. These include would-be appellants denied legal aid but wanting a second opinion; and complaints about disciplinary hearings, interference with correspondence, limitations in access to lawyers, and the use of a transfer from one prison to another as a form of punishment.

Two cases handled by NCCL in 1982 indicate the nature of the Council's prison work. In the *Santara* case, NCCL argued against the double jeopardy of prisoners who, under an earlier Court of Appeal ruling, are liable to punishment both under internal prison discipline and under the criminal law. In the *Grainger* case an (unsuccessful) attempt was made to challenge the validity of a governor's disciplinary hearing, which denied the prisoner's request to call a witness.

POLICING AND THE ADMINISTRATION OF JUSTICE

In the early morning of Saturday 22 April 1972, firemen were called to 27 Doggett Road in Catford, South London. The fire was extinguished in under 10 minutes; in a room at the top of the house, which had not been scorched by the blaze, the strangled body of a male prostitute, Maxwell Confait, was discovered. The events which followed directly inspired a re-examination of some aspects of the administration of justice, and also brought to light one of the most notorious examples of its maladministration.

Very quickly, 3 youths were arrested: Ronnie Leighton aged 15, Ahmet Salih aged 14, and Colin Lattimore aged 18 but with a mental age of 8. As a result of confessions which they made to the police under questioning, the three were convicted in November of various offences including arson, manslaughter and murder. There were, however, several disturbing features of the case which led many people, including Lattimore's parents and, later, Christopher Price (then MP for Lewisham West), to regard the convictions as unsafe. First, the Judges' Rules and Administrative Directions had been breached. These Rules, which do not have the force of law, have been drawn up as guidelines for police in their questioning of suspects and witnesses. They lay down, for example, that the police must caution suspects, and in a particular way; that reasonable arrangements are made for comfort; that written statements are made on official forms, and so on. The Confait confessions breached at least one of the Rules: that those under 17 should, as far as possible, only be questioned in the presence of a parent or someone not a police officer who is of the same sex as the person questioned. In this case, all three youths were questioned without the presence of any independent witnesses, lawyers, or parents. They also claimed that they had been frightened into making their confessions, which could not therefore be thought of as properly voluntary. But judges have the discretion to decide that statement can be treated as admissible evidence even where it is established that there has been a breach of the Rules.

A second disturbing feature of the case was the treatment of the medical evidence. At the trial, the police surgeon placed the time of death as between 8 pm and 10 pm on 21 April; the Crown's pathologist offered the time as between 6.30 pm and 11.45 pm. Even with the second, wider, possibility, it looked as though the accused would be acquitted because Lattimore – the alleged strangler – had a firm alibi during these hours. The prosecution could only succeed if it cast doubt on this medical evidence, and emphasised the importance of the confessions. They asked the jury to accept that, contrary to the doctors' opinion, Confait had been murdered in the hour after midnight. The problem with this hypothesis was that, when Confait's body was found at 1.23 am, it exhibited signs of *rigor mortis*; but as *rigor* does not usually set in until 5 or 6 hours after death, this evidence also suggested a time of death consistent with the estimates of the two doctors. Mr Justice Chapman attempted to get over this difficulty in his summing up by suggesting that the heat from the fire might have accelerated *rigor* in Confait's body and brought it on within an hour of his death.

Lattimore's parents got in touch with NCCL early in 1974, and a pathologist, Professor Donald Teare, was brought in. He too placed the time of death at between 8 pm and 10 pm, and dismissed the judge's theory about *rigor* as 'without any scientific background whatsoever'.[15] One of the Council's legal volunteers, Jonathan Caplan, who was closely concerned with the case, noted other worrying circumstances surrounding the convictions:

One of the officers admitted in court that he had deliberately falsified his official notebook for that fateful Monday evening, the night of the questioning. Medical evidence showed that Lattimore was extremely suggestible and was prepared to agree to almost any question put to him. There was not a single piece of corroborative evidence to support the alleged confessions. A statement from the wife of Confait's landlord (a fellow transvestite who was in love with Confait), implicating her husband with the murder, was withheld from the defence lawyers and, having only accidentally come to light during the trial, cross-examination upon it was heavily restricted on the grounds of irrelevance.[16]

Christopher Price campaigned tirelessly for a review of the case. The Court of Appeal had already dismissed an appeal, and the Home Secretary will only refer cases back to the Court of Appeal if there is fresh evidence. In the end, it was probably the publicity rather than the arguments which led to the case being referred, and in 1975, 3 years after the youths had been sentenced, the convictions were quashed.

Sir Henry Fisher was appointed by the Home Secretary to enquire into this gross miscarriage of justice, and his report was complete by the end of 1977. Fisher criticised the police for questioning Leighton and Salih without the presence of a parent; he found that the questioning of Lattimore was 'unfair and oppressive'; the pathologist retained by the coroner was criticised for failing to take Confait's rectal temperature at the scene of death – had he done so, Fisher thought that this 'might well have altered the whole course of the case'. There was a conspiracy to fudge the central issue: 'those concerned with the investigation and prosecution . . . made every effort to keep the time of death as vague as possible'.[17]

The most important finding concerned Direction 7 of the Rules. It requires that those in custody be told of their right to telephone a lawyer or friend, and to consult a solicitor in private, provided that the investigation is not, thereby, unreasonably delayed. Notices must be posted in police stations giving this information. Fisher's discovery here was staggering: 'The existence of Administrative Direction 7 was unknown to counsel and to senior police officers who gave evidence before me. In the Metropolitan Police District it is not observed.'[18]

The Fisher Report concluded with the recommendation that confessions should be excluded automatically if, first, they were obtained in breach of the Rules; secondly, if made by children in the absence of parents or independent witnesses; and thirdly, if made by mentally handicapped persons. The government, instead of legislating, prevaricated by setting up a Royal Commission on Criminal Procedure, under Sir Cyril Phillips. NCCL gave extensive written and oral evidence to this body. However, when the Commission finally reported, its response to Fisher was, from the libertarian perspective, signally disappointing. Confession statements would not be excluded using the Fisher criteria, but only if they had been obtained by torture, inhuman or degrading treatment, violence or the threat of violence.

With regard to the Judges' Rules, Phillips suggested replacing them with a code of practice to be drawn up by the Home Office. The chief weakness here was that there was no explanation of how the new code would be enforced; if it was to be merely for guidance, like the old Rules, then this was hardly a significant step towards reform.

After the Royal Commission, the Conservative government introduced the Police and Criminal Evidence Bill which, but for the general election of 1983, would almost certainly have passed into law. (At the time of writing, December 1983, an altered version of the Bill – pretending to be free of those anti-libertarian elements which attracted such cross-party condemnation in the original Bill – is about to go through its various Parliamentary stages.) Clause 60 of the Bill set out yet another group of unsatisfactory proposals. Confessions would be excluded if they were obtained by oppression (basically the Phillips criteria) or, and here was a new formula, in consequence of anything said or done which would render them unreliable. This looked like an adequately wide safeguard, but NCCL's ex-chairperson Peter Thornton explained his misgivings. The new arrangements would allow a judge, in reaching a decision as to the admissibility of a confession statement, to take into account its likely truth or falsity; under the old arrangements, regard could only be had to the circumstances under which it was made. Thornton reiterated NCCL's long-standing insistence that only a statutory exclusion of all confessions obtained in breach of the Rules would do. As for the new formula: 'Clause 60 is not only a muddle, it is a dangerous muddle.'[19] More than a decade after Confait's death, the story is yet unfinished.

The Council's somewhat misleading public image, as a body primarily concerned with police malpractice, has resulted in its being the recipient of a flood of allegations against the police. It has therefore taken a lively interest in the reform of the police complaints' procedure. Prior to 1976, this was entirely an internal police matter. Yet NCCL gave a very cool welcome to the 1976 Police Act which purported to introduce an independent element into the system.

The Act laid down that every complaint must be recorded and investigated and, if necessary, internal disciplinary action taken. If the complaint alleges a criminal offence, then the papers are automatically sent to the Director of Public Prosecutions unless the deputy chief constable is satisfied that the alleged offence has not been committed. In deciding whether or not to prosecute individual police officers, the Director applies the celebrated '50 per cent' rule; if, on the available evidence, there is at least a 50 per cent chance of securing a conviction, then a prosecution is instituted. However, in certain cases, the Director may exercise a discretion not to prosecute, even if the 50 per cent rule is satisfied, if it is felt that a prosecution would not be in the public interest. For example, it might be thought wasteful of public funds to proceed with a case against an officer who is about to retire, or has resigned from the force, or has become terminally ill.

In these two respects – the 50 per cent rule, and the discretion to refrain from prosecution – a police officer and a member of the public are theoretically in the same position *viz* the Director. In practice, however, the officer is at an advantage because, as it is well established that juries convict officers with greater reluctance than members of the public, it follows that the evidence of wrongdoing by a police officer will have to be stronger than in other cases in order to satisfy the 50 per cent rule.

The Director communicates the decision about prosecution back to the deputy chief constable, who then decides whether any disciplinary charges should be brought against the accused. This decision is then sent to the Police Complaints Board, the body set up under the 1976 Act to inject a supposedly independent element into the whole system. The Board can disagree with the deputy chief constable's decision not to institute disciplinary proceedings, and can insist that they take place.

This complaints' system has serious weaknesses. First, the Board rarely flexes its muscles. Between 1977 and 1981, it disagreed with a deputy in only 77 cases. Secondly, the Board itself expressed a specific dissatisfaction, in July 1980, when it recorded its fear that, in the investigation of complaints of serious injury, the investigators might be too disposed to favour the evidence of the accused over that of the complainant. Thirdly, even in serious cases where officers from outside forces are called in to investigate, police officers are still investigating each other, and the inevitable loyalty amongst them (especially strong in socially isolated and quasi-military peer groups like the police) leads to public suspicion of a lack of rigour in the enquiries. Even the Police Federation conceded this point in 1982: 'there appears to be no way in which the public will be convinced of the fairness of the system so long as the police appear to be judges in their own courts'.[20] It is also backed up by the Home Office's own research unit which, on studying its complaint files for the 1970s, found that there were many examples of lack of investigative thoroughness; and by an *Observer* opinion poll which showed that less than half those questioned were happy with the complaints' procedure. Fourthly, the procedure is extraordinarily cumbersome; its long-winded formality and rigidity allows for no mechanism of conciliation. Fifthly, little effort is made to keep the complainant properly informed of the course of the investigation; it is common for such a complainant, after very many months, simply to receive notification that the complaint has been found to be 'unsubstantiated', without any accompanying explanation. This perfunctoriness does damage to police–community relations.

However, perhaps the most debated and complicated feature of the present arrangements concerns the 'double jeopardy' rule. It is a basic tenet of English law that no one should be tried twice for the same offence; that is to say, they should not be placed in double jeopardy. As applied to police officers, this concept works in the following way. Obviously, an officer can face disciplinary proceedings without the Director of Public Prosecutions being involved at all, if the alleged offence is not criminal. Also, after being prosecuted and acquitted, an officer can then face internal discipline as well. The real weakness is revealed in those cases where the officer is reported to the Director, and a decision not to prosecute is taken. If the Director's decision is based on an insufficiency of evidence (rather than, say, considerations of compassion or public policy) then Home Office guidelines say that there should not normally be disciplinary charges as well. This produces some situations in which no action is taken at all, even though it is accepted on all sides that an injustice has occurred. Such a case Patricia Hewitt describes:

> Errol Madden, a black 17-year-old, was walking home late one night when he was arrested on suspicion of theft. He was taken to the police station, where two officers searched his

bag, in which they found two model toys – bought by Errol earlier that week as models for his painting course. After several hours' questioning, during which, Errol says, he was racially abused and threatened, Errol signed a 'confession' statement written out by one of the officers admitting that he had stolen his own model toys. In fact, the receipt for one of the toys was in the bag! NCCL represented Errol and ensured that the charges against him were dropped. His complaint against the police was investigated by the Metropolitan Police's Complaints Investigation Bureau, and referred to the DPP for possible charges of conspiracy to pervert the course of justice against the two arresting officers. The DPP declined to prosecute. And the Board wrote to Errol saying that although Errol was subjected to 'some distinctly unprofessional behaviour on the part of the police' and that his treatment 'reflects very badly on the Metropolitan Police', the 'double jeopardy' rule made it impossible for them to press disciplinary charges. Thus, the officers against whom the most serious complaints were made faced no action whatsoever.[21]

On 21 December 1982, in the Divisional Court, Mr Justice McNeill quashed this decision of the Police Complaints Board, saying that the Board had misinterpreted a particular section of the Police Act 1976; they had wrongly applied the double jeopardy rule, and it would be necessary for them to consider afresh whether, although the DPP had declined to prosecute, the police officers involved in the arrest and questioning of Madden should be subject to disciplinary proceedings. This legal reversal was a victory for the Council; in particular, it showed how the strategy of adopting carefully selected test cases was paying dividends.

The Council is currently proposing a complete overhaul of the complaints procedure. In the NCCL plan, the Complaints Board would take a far more important role; it would have a network of regional offices and, most important of all, would have its own investigators who would not be police officers. It has repeatedly been claimed by those opposed to an independent investigative force that such a force would lack the necessary skill. Only the police have the expertise to investigate the police, it is said. But many public bodies have their own teams of investigators, which operate successfully: for example, the Home Office Immigration Service, the Inland Revenue, British Rail, London Transport, Customs and Excise, and the Atomic Energy Authority.

The NCCL proposals also envisage a conciliation service to reduce the daunting formality of current practice. Such proposals, if implemented, will lead to greater public confidence in the police service and, in so far as this will in turn lead to more successful policing, is clearly in the interests of the police themselves.

INFORMATION

Right at the beginning of Patricia Hewitt's incumbency as general secretary, NCCL found itself in the extraordinary position of buying five million personal files for one penny. The story went back six years, to the time in February 1969 when two directors of Tracing Services Ltd were each fined £5,000 for conspiring to effect a public mischief (an offence which, later on, the House of Lords, in the *Withers* case, decided did not exist!) The directors of TSL had hired people to act as imposters; bogus doctors, policemen and tax officials went around successfully obtaining confidential information, which was then recorded on personal files. TSL went bust in 1974, and the files were bought by a firm called Konfax Ltd, who eventually sold them to the Council with the proviso that they be destroyed. The whole bizarre affair illustrated the ease with which confidential information could be obtained improperly;

how, once acquired, it could fall into the hands of any purchaser, without safeguards; and how all this could take place with very little effective legal remedy.

The Council's increasing concern about the use to which computers could be put led to its organising, with the Parliamentary Civil Liberties Group, a meeting for MPs, addressed by computer experts, on 22 April 1969. In the same year, NCCL held discussions with people in the computer industry, and was rather surprised to find a great deal of support for its position from that quarter. *Computer Weekly*, for example, spelt out the threats to privacy in the use of data banks for working the earnings-related pension scheme. NCCL also took part in an international Data Fair in Manchester, which addressed itself to the ethical, legal, and technical aspects of information storage. Joe Jacob, a lecturer in law and a member of the Council's executive, contributed to the debate in a widely-circulated NCCL paper called *Data Banks, the Computer and the Law*.

1969 also saw considerable NCCL activity on the legislative front. A delegation (including MPs Eric Lubbock and Kenneth Baker, and Lord Windlesham) met the Minister of Health, David Ennals, and later in the year, largely as a result of the Council's circulating to MPs a draft Bill, Brian Walden introduced a Private Members' Bill on the Right to Privacy. Although in itself unsuccessful, it was instrumental in convincing the government to set up the Younger Committee on privacy in 1970. It reported in 1972, and recommended that information should be kept for specific purposes only; that access to it should be limited; that the subject of the information should know of the records kept and have the opportunity of correcting them; that there should be a time limit for information retention; and that subjective opinions in the records should be treated with special care.

In 1975, the Law Commission responded to Younger by suggesting that the civil offence of 'breach of confidence' could be expanded to protect privacy. They argued that a person who suffered distress or financial loss through a breach of confidence, should have the right to sue. In the same year the government issued two White Papers, and set up the Data Protection Committee, which in turn was to recommend the best way of setting up a Data Protection Authority. This committee, chaired by Norman Lindop, suggested that legally enforceable codes of practice be drawn up by the Data Protection Authority, which was to be an independent body with powers to investigate complaints and enforce the law. In 1982 another White Paper appeared; the DPA idea was rejected in favour of a Data Registrar who would supervise the new arrangements, summarised here by Ruth Cohen:

> All users of data systems which automatically process information relating to identifiable individuals would be required to register but an unspecified number of 'special cases and exemptions' would be allowed. Subject to these, central and local government, the police, nationalized industries and other public bodies would be required to register in the same way as other users. The Codes of Practice, recommended in the Lindop Report, were downgraded in the White Paper to voluntary codes of guidance which might be prepared by 'some professional bodies, trade associations and other organisations' but they would not be legally enforceable. However, some regulations might be needed for particular categories of data, for instance, medical records.[22]

NCCL had major reservations about the new proposals, and these were set out in September 1982.[23] First, and most important, only computerised data was affected; manual records were to be exempt from the new regulations. But the majority of complaints received by the Council concerned precisely these manual records: files kept on schoolchildren, on employees in offices and factories, on hospital patients, on DHSS claimants. Furthermore, those holding manual records would be reluctant to computerise them because they would thus place themselves within the legal restrictions. The law, therefore, would act as a disincentive to modernisation.

The proposal that sections of the police, other law enforcement bodies, and the security services, be allowed exemption from the need to register was also attacked. It was argued that the mere fact of knowing basic details about police computers – the amount of information held, for example, and the way it was classified – could not be said to constitute a danger to national security or crime prevention. It was suggested that, to reassure the public of the Registrar's independence, the person appointed should not be a present or former civil servant. Also, that the Registrar's functions were too circumscribed; the White Paper's admission that 'he will not have the resources to supervise the operation of data systems in detail'[24] should be replaced by a plan to give her/him greater powers of investigation and supervision.

The rejection of statutory codes of practice, as recommended by Lindop, for voluntary ones, was a great weakness. Many firms would ignore them if they were unenforceable. The White Paper did suggest restrictive regulations for specially sensitive information (for example, on sexual life, criminal convictions, political affiliations) but it looked as though the body drawing up these regulations would be precisely that body whose various departments would be keeping the records – the Home Office. Even the subject's access to computerised records was restricted, where the information was held for reasons of security, crime prevention, or as medical or social work information.

Whilst accepting some restrictions, NCCL argued in particular against closed access for medical records, citing an Australian hospital, the Royal Melbourne, where patients' access to their medical records had proved successful. Finally, NCCL urged that there should be criminal sanctions for use against those who broke the most serious regulations, and that a legal duty of confidentiality should be placed on keepers of data. Patricia Hewitt recognised that here was one of those rare occasions when the business community and the libertarian were at one: '. . . the failure of successive British Governments to legislate for data protection not only threatens the rights and interests of individual citizens, but also places British firms at a serious disadvantage when competing for contracts which involve the transfer of personal data across national borders. Human rights and commercial interests point to the urgent need for data protection legislation'.[25]

One piece of useful legislation which had already been passed was the Consumer Credit Act 1974, which came into force in 1977. This gives everyone a right to see their credit reference file; if the company in question fails to comply, they can be prosecuted and fined up to £200. But it was small beer for NCCL who, in the same year the CCA became effective, launched a major 'Right to Know' campaign, based on a Council report by Hewitt called *Privacy: the Information Gatherers*.[26] The report illustrated the consequence of the misuse of data: DHSS claimants being described as 'neurotic', political opinions being recorded, and a couple refused credit because a previous lodger in the same house had been a debt defaulter. All manner of absurdities and gross errors were unearthed.

After the report's publication, NCCL continued of course to publicise and in many instances give active support to individual cases. One NCCL member reported that the Granada TV Rental company had asked him for 19 separate pieces of personal information, including details of his mortgage, driving licence, banker's card, two credit accounts and a reference! Early in 1978, the Council opposed the Tameside Housing Department's proposed secret classification of council tenants. Families were to be described as 'very good', 'reasonable', 'below average' or 'unsuitable', and only those in the first two categories would be eligible for transfer to the more desirable estates. NCCL acquired copies of two Tameside Council meetings, which made it clear that the tenants themselves would be kept in the dark about their classification rating, the criteria for which would be 'based on the degree of cleanliness, maintenance of payments of rent and general social attitude'.[27]

This last criterion seemed to be the most objectionable because so absurdly vague: 'Why should someone's "general social attitude" be relevant to their housing? Or will this become a façade for prejudice – against unmarried mothers, gays, West Indians or Asians, militants . . .'.[28]

The Welge case was even more alarming. Hans Welge had accepted a paint spraying job with the Kennings Motor Group in Colchester, in 1979. The firm insisted on insuring all its employees, but the insurance firm refused to write a policy for Welge, as a result of which he was sacked. As the reasons for refusal had nothing to do with credit rating, Welge had no legal right to see the (mis?) information on which the refusal was based. He was unable to bring defamation proceedings against the insurance company because he could not afford the legal fees; defamation does not qualify for legal aid, even if it results in consequences as serious as the loss of a job.

More controversial than the Council's work on manual and computerised records was its endeavour to secure freedom of information in the public domain, and to see the repeal of the Official Secrets Act 1911. As with prisons, there was a political consensus from left and right which recognised the nonsense of the existing arrangements; indeed, even the pro-establishment *Sunday Telegraph* found two of its staff, Brian Roberts and Jonathan Aitken, in the dock in 1970, for publishing Foreign Office documents on the Biafran war. They were acquitted, and Mr Justice Caufield allowed himself to remark that the case 'may well alert those who govern us at least to consider . . . whether Section 2 of this Act has reached retirement age and should be pensioned off'.[29]

Like so much legislation, the OSA had been passed for one set of purposes and was consistently used for others. It had originally been rushed through as an emergency measure; section one designed to prevent espionage prejudicial to the state, and section two concerned with secret government information. But what did secret mean? In 1971, the Franks Committee gave an alarmingly wide answer: 'It is an official secret if it is in an official file.'[30] Prosecutions were often politically sensitive, and often dropped for that reason. In 1974 two people were charged with possessing a Ministry of Defence manual called, *Land Operations, Vol. 3: Counter Revolutionary Operations*; 2 years earlier, the editor of the *Railway Gazette* was charged after publishing details of proposed rail cuts; in both cases, the prosecution was withdrawn.

In December 1977, 39 years after their previous attempt, the National Union of Journalists and the Council held another conference as part of the campaign for repeal of the OSA. The conference heard from the writer and barrister James Michael of the advantages of the USA's Freedom of Information Act; legislation on similar lines in the UK would turn the tables completely. Instead of its being an offence merely to possess certain information, it would be a legal obligation on most public bodies to supply it on demand, always granted obvious safeguards. It was, therefore, an unfortunate setback when Clement Freud's Official Information Bill, based on the American model and backed by NCCL, was defeated in March 1979. The same year saw the publication by the Council of James Michael's *The Politics of Secrecy*, a closely-argued study of the nature and extent of official secrecy, and the viability of diferent legislative proposals for reform. The chief reason for the failure of Parliament to bring about reform was, for Michael, only too obvious: 'both those who hold office and those who think they are likely to win it want to retain control over information about how power is exercised'.[31] In the immediate future, access to data, whether in personal files concerning individuals, or state papers dealing with governmental decisions, looks like being a major NCCL priority.

GAY RIGHTS

In its recent history, NCCL has from time to time passed impeccably liberal motions on gay rights. But in the fifties, the publication of the Wolfenden Report (1957) did not see the Council itself in any campaign for legislation. Only since the mid-1970s has the organisation adopted a more positive role. It has in particular concerned itself with job discrimination against gay people.

One of the first employment cases which NCCL took up was that of John Warburton, a London teacher banned from ILEA schools after he had refused to give an undertaking not to discuss homosexuality in class. Warburton was spotted on a gay rights' march by a pupil, and the following Monday was met with sexist remarks from a group of pupils in class. The only way to deal with the hostility was to discuss it with the pupils, but the hysteria about sexuality which so characterises Christian Britain resulted in ILEA insisting on their ban.

Veronica Pickles found that her secondment for a health visitor's training course was withdrawn once her campaigning work with the Milton Keynes Campaign for Homosexual Equality group came to notice. NCCL wrote to the authorities, denouncing the action as a pandering to prejudice. The Council received a reply which stated that Pickles would have been treated the same 'had she been involved in some other matter of social controversy and of a nature likely to weaken patients' confidence in her'.[32] It was signed, on behalf of the DHSS, by Michael Meacher. In 1975, NCCL represented Pickles in her appeal against dismissal; she won the case.

In February 1981, a drama lecturer at Salford College was dismissed following a conviction for gross indecency; this 'offence' involved consensual activity behind locked doors. But because the doors were those of a public lavatory, and the law considers it a 'public' place, Gordon Wiseman was convicted. His appeal was rejected by the Employment Appeal Tribunal, but a dissenting voice on the EAT remarked that ". . . it is helpful to gain a perspective by asking the question "Would a male or female heterosexual lecturer have been dismissed if discovered soliciting or indulging in promiscuous behaviour?" '[33]

In terms of legal precedent, the most important employment case of the period has been that of John Saunders, sacked from his job as a maintenance worker by the Scottish National Camps Association. Saunders had not committed any offence at all; his employers simply sacked him for *being* gay. In the letter of dismissal they wrote: 'At a camp accommodating large numbers of schoolchildren and teenagers it is totally unsuitable to employ any persons with such tendencies.'[34] When the case reached the EAT, that body decided that employers were entitled to dismiss workers on the basis of a prejudice widely held by 'reasonable' people, even if it could be established that the prejudice in question had no substance in fact. This proposition was so astonishing that even *The Times* was aghast. Bernard Levin wrote: 'if he does not get legal redress it will have been judicially established that a citizen who is wholly blameless may be punished because some people believe that *other* people, not including the citizen in question, might, in certain circumstances, behave wrongly'.[35]

These fears were realised when *Saunders* was cited as a precedent by an employer who had dismissed an epileptic, under the widely-held but erroneous view that epilepsy constitutes a bar to being a good employee.

The legal status of gay parents is little better than that of gay employees. When the custody of children is contested, the law automatically assumes that the child will be better off with a heterosexual parent. In the leading case of *re D (an infant) (1977)* the various pronouncements of their lordships give a clear indication of the typical approach of most judges to custody and access issues. Lord Wilberforce allowed himself to remark:

Whatever new attitudes parliament, or public tolerance, may have chosen to take as regards the behaviour of consenting adults over 21, these should not entitle the courts to relax, in any degree, the vigilance and severity with which they should regard the risk of children, at critical ages being exposed or introduced to ways of life which, as this case illustrates, may lead to severance from normal society, to psychological stresses and unhappiness . . .[36]

That such severance, stresses and unhappiness are actually produced by people like Wilberforce administering unjust laws does not seem to occur to him.

Most custody disputes concern lesbian mothers. In his authoritative *Gays and the Law*, Paul Crane sets the scene for these hearings:

> . . . every facet of her life is open to scrutiny . . . it is common . . . to ask questions about the gay parents' sexual partners, about the amount of affection the parent shows to a lover while the children are present, whether the parent is active in feminist or gay organizations, whether the children play with the toys 'appropriate' to their biological sex and even whether or not they share a bed.
>
> Judges and lawyers will often insinuate or directly accuse lesbian parents of molesting their own children, of not caring about them, or of having sexual relations in front of their children. The affront to a parent's dignity is constant throughout the court proceedings.[37]

In some court cases, it has actually been said that children should be separated from their parents so as to avoid the children's potential embarrassment at having a gay mother or father! There is, however, a tiny light showing in the darkness. In February 1983, the Court of Appeal awarded custody of two sisters to their lesbian mother and her lover rather than to their father and his new wife; a decision supported by the welfare officers.

One of the most important legal cases of recent years, and one in which the Council lent support, was that brought by Jeff Dudgeon against the British government on the grounds that the law as it then was in Northern Ireland infringed his rights. The Sexual Offences Act of 1967 (which introduced a limited liberalisation of the law by permitting homosexual acts be-

tween consenting male adults over 21 in private, provided that
they were not forces personnel or merchant seamen) did not
apply to Northern Ireland, where all such acts were wholly
illegal between men. (Gay women were never criminalised.) By
a majority of 15 to 4, the judges of the European Court of
Human Rights held, on 22 October 1981, that this position was
an infringement of the Convention on Human Rights insofar as
it constituted a violation of the 'right to respect for private life'.
An unfortunate aspect of the judgement was that the Court
upheld the right of governments to have regard to religious
sentiment in the framing of legislation, which has the regret-
table effect of conferring respectability on what is merely a
pandering to the half-baked prejudice of zealots. (Before the
ruling, Ian Paisley had mounted a 'Save Ulster from Sodomy'
campaign, and the Roman Catholic hierarchy was also active
in spreading homophobia. Here at last was something the two
communities could come together about.)

The Dudgeon case led to the extension of the 1967 Act to
Northern Ireland; but, although better than nothing, the Act
still represents a grave injustice, most especially to all those
under 21 who are branded with criminality if they seek to
express their love, and who in any case have to contend with the
discrimination which is actively encouraged by such legislation. The two largest political parties still remain uncommitted
to full legal equality (Labour want initially to reduce the age of
consent to 18; it is 16 for heterosexuals).

In the 1980s, the Council has been able to employ a Gay
Rights' Officer; the first incumbent was Barry Prothero,
succeeded by Anne Marie-Bradley. At the moment, funds
prevent a replacement of the latter, who left in 1983, but as a
result of a GLC grant, NCCL has been able to take on, for 18
months, a researcher (Sam Jenkins) for the Gay Community
Policing Project. The aim of the project is to monitor police
harassment of the gay community, and to report on any
positive developments in relations with the police when they
occur. A recent issue of *Rights* contains precisely the sort of
incident which the project will be monitoring. One Sunday

lunchtime in October 1982, a youth worker, intent on catching up with some work, went to his place of work on the second floor of an office building:

> Upon opening the front door he was surprised to see a large wicker basket full of overalls, tapes and assorted equipment [and] in another room, two men in overalls operating video cameras.
>
> The men identified themselves as policemen and asked the youth worker to keep quiet about their presence as they were filming the street in an operation designed to catch muggers. This seemed a somewhat odd exercise at noon on a Sunday and the youth worker specifically noticed that the surveillance camera was pointed at a local pub and that record sheets were headed with the name of the pub. This pub is a well known meeting place for members of the gay community.[38]

In 1982, the Council protested to the BBC about its many homophobic attitudes, but in particular about two issues. First were the routine slurs (e.g. Bernard Falk's reference to 'effeminate poofs' on Radio 4's *Breakaway*, and Robert Robinson's description of gay people as 'horrific and paranoid' on *Stop the Week*) from which the corporation, apparently as a matter of policy, exempts other minority groups. The second main complaint was over the BBC's continued and outrageous refusal to allow any gay spokespersons to appear on *Any Questions* or *Question Time*.

In public debates, the BBC repeatedly falls back on one standard argument when it is accused of bias. It is claimed that the corporation acts as a 'window on the world', that it merely reflects what the world is like rather than pushing the audience towards one interpretation of its events. But the policy of excluding gay people from discussion, and then ridiculing them in their absence, proves once and for all the nonsense of the 'reflection' theory. The insistence by the BBC that only heterosexuals, or closet homosexuals, may argue points, hardly leads to a 'reflection' of all shades of opinion. When the Pope came to Britain, no gay spokespersons were invited to counter-balance his bigotry; only heterosexuals were allowed to voice ideas about Catholic teachings. The extraordinary distortion by which the Ambridge of *The Archers* has a 100 per cent heterosexual population, is hardly a reflection of reality. The blocking of telephoned questions on gay rights' issues on Radio 4's *Election Call* programme during the 1983 general election was only a more conspicuous example of a mentality which operates throughout the year and in all departments of the corporation. The notorious way in which the BBC insists that its gay comedians deny their sexual orientation in public interviews, so that the subsequent ridiculing of homosexuals in the comedy sketches in which such actors participate will be doubly humiliating, is yet another example of the heterosexism.

Some of these points were made in NCCL's protest letter of 1982. The then Chairman of the BBC, George Howard, merely brushed them aside without giving a single undertaking for the future. (Rather amusingly, he denied that Bernard Falk had made the remark quoted above, a remark for which Mark Bonham-Carter, in a letter on 21 May 1981, had already apologised.) Nor is the future reassuring; for if Bonham-Carter was illiberal as Vice-Chairman, Sir William Rees-Mogg is considerably worse. As ex-editor of *The Times*, he is an old hand at fighting rear-guard actions against legal equality for gay people. The chances that such a man will use his Vice-Chairmanship to prevent change and reform are great. The chances that under him the public will be able to see and hear programmes which are a positive and joyful celebration and affirmation of gay lifestyles, is nil. (One should note in passing that the BBC is not exclusively culpable. Channel 4, which at its inception promised to provide programmes with a positive perspective on homosexuality, has totally retreated from that position and not only fails to make specifically 'gay' programmes to parallel their output for smaller minorities, but in its supposedly socially-aware *Brookside* serial, they too have followed the BBC lead, and created the ludicrous situation of an entirely heterosexual set of fictional characters.)

It is important to understand that homophobia is by no means a preserve of the political right in broadcasting and journalism. The *Spectator* may now be something of a joke (albeit a tired one) with its Waugh–Ingrams team pumping out venom by the week, but the recent *New Statesman* under Bruce Page's editorship matched its rival with almost as many sneers at 'poofs' and 'pansies'. *Time Out* can still (1983) get away with reviewing the film-maker Fassbinder as a 'drug-crazed German faggot', and, in the early days, the *Spare Rib* collective's sexist antagonism towards gay women was disgraceful.

Whether media bigotry and misrepresentation of this kind – we shall see equally exceptionable examples in the response to the Council's work on sexual harassment – can be handled at all by a civil liberties' organisation like NCCL is open to doubt. In recent years, members of the executive committee have addressed themselves to the problem of reconciling the principle of freedom of the media, with the knowledge that abuse of that freedom leads in turn to an illiberal society. The old Pritt–Kidd debate again. It may be that we will have to accept that a free press and free broadcasting will almost always mean a predominantly illiberal one reflecting the minority views of rich proprietors and establishment stooges.

At the moment, the gay rights sub-committee of NCCL is prioritising issues which are of equal concern to gay women and men: gay parents' custody; immigration rules; and of course, policing policy.

WOMEN'S RIGHTS

In 1973, the emergence of the women's movement as a conscious force was reflected within NCCL; a women's rights sub-committee was set up, and in September Patricia Hewitt started work as the Cobden Trust's women's rights officer. Almost at once a conference was held, bringing together women from all over the country, trade unionists as well as the newer women's groups. A pamphlet entitled *Danger: Women at Work* resulted, and a women's rights page became a regular feature of *Civil Liberty*.

The issue of 'foreign husbands' produced an NCCL campaign which allied concern about unjust racialist immigration laws with anger at the unequal treatment accorded to women. British nationality law arose from the premise that a married woman was not a person in her own right, but an appendage of her husband, and that she therefore lost her own citizenship to take on his – even if he did not have one! In 1948, NCCL advised a British-born woman who had married a Polish subject. He later lost his nationality, becoming a stateless person, and she claimed the right to revert to the British nationality she had acquired at birth. The Passport Office, however, advised her that she had irretrievably lost her own nationality on marriage.

The 1971 Immigration Act confirmed the view that a woman had no entitlement to nationality in her own right. Until 1968, women married to foreign men had at least had the right to bring their husbands to Britain with them. But in that year the Labour Government, fearing that Asian men might thereby gain entitlement to residence by means of marriages of convenience, removed that right. Despite the racialist intent of this move, the ban extended to all British women with foreign husbands. The response to NCCL's campaign against the ban was therefore very widespread, involving women's organisations, ethnic minority groups and labour movement bodies, as well as many outraged individuals. In November 1974, *Civil Liberty* was able to announce that the campaign had won a partial success and that a woman with the right to settle in the UK could now bring her husband with her.

Victory was short-lived. By the end of the decade the question was re-opened, when the government undertook a radical overhaul of the law on immigration and nationality. The resultant Act recognised that it was blatantly discriminatory to allow wives of British men to become British immediately, while requiring a delay of 5 years before husbands of British women could obtain naturalisation on these grounds. This was resolved by imposing a 3-year delay on all foreign spouses.

Meanwhile, the rules were altered so that a British woman could be joined in the UK by her foreign husband only if she, or one of her parents, had been born in the UK. This placed some British women in the paradoxical position whereby the only country in the EEC in which they did not have the right to reside with their husbands was Britain. NCCL has repeatedly challenged the Home Office on this issue, referring to the European Commission of Human Rights' cases which illustrate how the rules, by discrimination on the grounds of sex, race, and national origin, breach the European Convention on Human Rights.

It was not only husbands who were left stranded by the fact that women could not convey their nationality to others. In the late seventies, NCCL received a number of enquiries from women afraid that their children would be born stateless. One such was Rosemary, a British woman working in Stockholm. She was not married to the American father of her child, which meant that the baby could not take his American citizenship, was not, simply by being born in Sweden, entitled to Swedish citizenship, and had no right to British citizenship, since this could not be inherited from the mother.

A campaign organised by NCCL, the Equal Opportunities Commission (EOC), and a number of MPs, culminated in a Private Member's Bill put forward by Jill Knight MP, to amend the law and so allow children to take their mother's nationality. Faced with this all-party onslaught, the Home Secretary, Merlyn Rees, announced on 7 February 1979 that he would henceforth normally use his discretionary power to register as a British citizen the child of a British woman born in the UK.

The 1981 Nationality Act added a further twist to the problem by depriving children born in the UK of the automatic entitlement to British citizenship.

Not only in the realm of immigrants but also in financial provision, successive governments have been attacked by NCCL for discriminating against women. An article in the November 1942 edition of *Civil Liberty*, entitled 'Bombs show no sex bias', complained of two rates of compensation being paid under the Personal Injuries (Civilian) Scheme 1941. The campaign was successful, and the discrimination against women removed.

However, in 1948, when the government introduced its social security scheme, it was based on the assumption that working women were a temporary phenomenon. NCCL seems to have been slow to realise the punitive effect of this false prophecy upon women, particularly married women. It was not until late 1976 that NCCL entered into an alliance with the Child Poverty Action Group to publish *The Unequal Breadwinner* and call for an end to this fundamental injustice.

Some of the most blatant areas of discrimination were removed, and many others abolished, in November 1983, when the government implemented an EEC directive on equal treatment. But only those areas most narrowly related to the directive were reformed.

The belief, once expressed in the words 'My wife and I are one person and I am that person', pervades the Income Tax system, and this too has been the target of an NCCL campaign. The insistence of the Inland Revenue on discussing a married woman's tax affairs with her husband rather than with the woman herself provoked enormous indignation. Articles in such publications as *Woman's Realm* produced a deluge of letters to the EOC, and the practice was discontinued. The underlying assumptions are, however, unchanged; a married man still enjoys tax advantages to enable him to 'support' his wife, however inappropriate this may be to the relationship between them.

In 1976, NCCL played a major role in taking a further step to help women battered by their partners. In that year Jo Richardson MP introduced, as a Private Member's Bill, the Domestic Violence Act 1977, which made it less difficult for such women to invoke the protection of the law. Previously, a woman could only obtain an injunction instructing her husband not to assault her if she had already taken steps towards a judicial separation or divorce. The new Act removed this requirement, and gave the police powers to enforce matrimonial injunctions.

The Equal Pay Act of 1970 (not due to be implemented until 1975) did not, of course, outlaw sex discrimination as such. A woman could scarcely benefit from entitlement to the same pay if she were unable to get the job in the first place. In 1974, dissatisfied with the government's proposals whereby sex discrimination would be outlawed only in the field of employment, and with broad exemptions, NCCL published its own Model Bill. This extended equal opportunities to housing and the provision of goods, facilities and services. It also provided for injunctions to be sought at an early stage in cases where discrimination was serious and prolonged, and for special anti-discrimination tribunals to hear employment cases. In the event, Parliament accepted NCCL's proposal to extend the law, but rejected its suggestions for enforcement, legislating instead for the use of the existing Industrial Tribunals and County Courts, and the unwieldy enforcement process through the EOC and its non-discrimination notices.

The legislation came into force in December 1975 and by April 1976, NCCL had dealt with over three hundred enquiries concerning discrimination on the grounds of sex or marriage. Some of these were clearly within the scope of the new Acts, like the case of Ms O, who was turned down as a driver for a holiday firm because it was claimed women drivers did not fit the image of an adventure tour; and that of Anna Coote and Tess Gill (each of whom was, in turn, chairperson of NCCL) who were refused drinks at the bar of El Vino's in Fleet Street. Other queries were about areas not covered by the law: nationality, cohabitation, taxation and so on.

A surprisingly fruitful section of the Sex Discrimination Act was that which dealt with indirect discrimination. In simple terms, this states that an employer must not treat one sex less favourably than the other by setting up conditions with which it will be more difficult for one sex to comply (by advertising, for example, 'Bar Staff wanted. Must look good in skirts.') NCCL supported Linda Price, who successfully argued that the Civil Service was discriminating indirectly against women by recruiting to the Executive Officer grade only people of 28 or under. This ruled out many women who attempt to return to a career in their mid-thirties, after taking time off to have a family. Another success arising from the same provision was the case of Sandra Powell and Brenda Clarke, described by Ann Sedley (NCCL Women's Rights Officer) as 'one of the most significant under the Sex Discrimination Act'.[39] Powell and Clarke were made redundant because they worked part-time, and their union (the Transport and General Workers Union) had agreed with the management that part-time workers should be made redundant before full-timers, regardless of length of service. NCCL argued that since all the male workers were full-time (and only some of the women were) while all the part-time workers were women, such an agreement was indirect sex discrimination, and the Employment Appeal Tribunal, in a decision of enormous importance for part-time workers, agreed.

The sex discrimination legislation has been a major focus of NCCL's women's rights work. But the gap between the average earnings of men and women remains, and the number of women in top jobs is still disproportionate. NCCL's response to this has been twofold. It produced proposals for amending the legislation, which were put to Parliament in the form of a Sex Equality Bill, in December 1983 by Jo Richardson MP, but unfortunately defeated. It also adopted an idea originating in the United States under the name of affirmative action. This recognised that legislating against discrimination was insufficient, and that some form of positive action was required. This should not mean discriminating against men at the point at which a candidate is selected, but rather enabling women to compete on more equal terms, by discovering what factors were preventing their advancement. For example, a firm with few women in top management posts might argue that women did not apply for these posts; but if a prerequisite for promotion was a residential training course, women might be prevented by family commitments from undertaking this. A positive action programme might then introduce an equivalent course to be undertaken on day release.

In July 1982, the Council issued a pamphlet on sexual harassment written by Ann Sedley and Melissa Benn.[40] Of particular importance is the authors' insistence on the complicity of the victims – women who feel powerless to stop the harassment and are forced to 'go along' with it. Thus, the relatively small number of official complaints does not reflect the real size of the problem: 'Those women who did not complain gave the following reasons: 52 per cent believed nothing would be done, 43 per cent felt it would be treated lightly or they would be ridiculed. Thirty per cent were afraid of being blamed or of other repercussions.'[41]

Such involuntary acceptance is so firmly a part of our structured view of sex that the advocacy by the authors of its opposite – active resistance – not surprisingly drew heavy fire from the gutter press. In particular, the press seized on the following suggestion, which occurs nowhere else in the booklet and is by no means at the centre of the authors' argument: 'You might find it useful to return like with like to show men what harassment feels like. For instance, pinning up a picture of naked men or whistling and grabbing at men. Some women do not want to use this tactic.'[42] These calm and moderate lines were translated into headlines of which the following are typical: 'If an office Romeo grabs you, grab him back' and 'Give the groper a grab in return office girls told.'[43] Several levels of misrepresentation can be seen in these headlines. First, what in the pamphlet is a decidedly minor part of the argument becomes, for Fleet Street, the main thesis. Secondly, the nouns used to refer to the harassers belong to the category of words suggesting sexual prowess and/or male attractiveness: 'an office Romeo'; 'Wolf at work – so watch it'; 'Dealing with Casanovas at a pinch';[44] whereas the reality for the victims is far from 'romantic' in the sense suggested. Thirdly, the rhetorical devices used in the headlines – note, for example, the two cases of strong alliteration – are designed to create a tone of facetious humour, which is ultimately dismissive. Thus, an attempt to publicise a source of real human distress is turned, by the media, into a cheap joke.

Sedley and Benn explore different solutions to the harassment problem. First, they suggest how trade unions can become more involved, and reproduce an excellent NALGO leaflet which other trade unionists could use as a basis for their own efforts. Secondly, they discuss the legal possibilities. These are not very promising in the UK as matters stand, but the fact that in the USA two waitresses were awarded $275 000 gives heart to those who believe that Britain follows transatlantic fashions sooner or later.

In 1983, Patricia Hewitt resigned as general secretary, in order to fight as a Parliamentary candidate in the general election. She has been replaced by Larry Gostin, who, until his appointment, was Visiting Fellow in Law and Psychiatry at Oxford University Centre for Criminological Research. He holds a doctorate in law and is a member of the New York bar. In the 1960s, he was prominent in the civil rights' movement, and has worked for the American Civil Liberties Union and the Centre on Law and Poverty. His special field has been mental health; in 1974, after a year on a Fullbright scholarship, he was appointed as the first legal officer of MIND (the National Association for Mental Health). Four years later he became MIND's legal director and brought a series of cases before the European Commission and the European Court of Human Rights. His writing has been extensive and influential; in particular his *A Human Condition* played a key role in the passing of the Mental Health (Amendment) Act 1982. With Larry

Gostin, NCCL goes forward confidently to meet the continuing threats to civil liberty.

Fifty years ago, when NCCL started, the authority of the state supported a system which was mean and unfair; it is so today. The most effective weapon in the arsenal of our opponents is the 'taken-for-grantedness' of the status quo. Many of the population – including those least favoured by the system – blindly accept that, basically, things are more or less as they should be. As a consequence, our fight will always be represented as peripheral or extreme. And that is why we should take to heart what Thomas Paine said in 1776, in *Common Sense*, about the fight for freedom: 'And however our eyes may be dazzled with snow, or our ears deceived by sound; however prejudice may warp our wills, or interest darken our understanding, the simple voice of nature and of reason will say, it is right.'

Appendix I: The Council for Academic Freedom and Democracy

Professor John Saville

What is striking about the tertiary sector of education is its conservatism and adherence to traditional values and methods of organisation. During the fifties, change had been minimal in curricula and in administration. Oxford and Cambridge dominated the university scene, and the snobbery that had long been associated with these two centres continued unchecked. The redbrick universities remained markedly provincial; professors and heads of departments still gathered unto themselves a great deal of power over the working lives of their colleagues, and much of it was exercised in an arbitrary fashion. The majority of the teaching staffs of universities and polytechnics continued to be excluded from any effective influence within their own institutions. Students, whether undergraduate or postgraduate, were not expected or thought capable of exercising any control over the subjects they were taught or the ways in which the teaching was conducted.

In these matters the new universities – Sussex was the first to be established – were to some extent innovators, both in respect of curricula and in university administration and organisation, although less in the latter than in the area of the curricula; but before 1968 the extent of their innovations was limited.

By the second half of the sixties, the expansion of student numbers and academic staff was considerable; and it continued, although at a slower rate, for the first half of the next decade. The deficiencies and problems of traditional teaching methods and of the very traditional ways of governing institutions of higher learning were partially concealed by the beneficial consequences of growth in most subjects and in most departments; and it was only the events in France in the summer of 1968 that brought to the surface a large number of academic, pedagogic and administrative problems. The explosion of student grievances found a response among academic staff, especially the younger ones. Tertiary education had a marked preponderance of those under 40 years of age, and there was exhibited a growing resentment at the continuation of old styles and old ways of academic government.

It would be an exaggeration to compare the radicalisation of academic staff with that of the student body as a whole; although both were to decline in their radicalism very sharply from the mid-seventies onwards. But the conflicts among the teaching groups between the radicals and conservatives, while not on the scale experienced in France and some other European countries, were nevertheless quite intense. And there was now an increasing number of cases of individual teachers who were being subjected to various kinds of pressures, including the ultimate sanction of dismissal.

It was against this background of change that a small group of radically-minded academics – of varying political persuasions and mostly middle-aged – decided that the time had come to establish a civil liberties organisation within the tertiary sector. The professional organisation, the Association of University Teachers (AUT) had remained for the most part in its traditional ways, and although it was to change a good deal in the decade which followed, at the end of the sixties it was still reluctant to take on difficult civil liberties' cases.

The group which came together in 1970 was centred on Professor John Griffith, professor of Public Law at the London School of Economics. Others present at the preliminary discussions included Ralph Miliband, John Westergaard and John Saville, the first two also at the LSE, and the last named at

Hull University. An early approach was made to the National Council for Civil Liberties, whose secretary was Tony Smythe, and from its beginnings the new body has been an independent but component part of NCCL. At the founding conference, the new body was named; and CAFD became the acronym for the Council for Academic Freedom and Democracy.

Almost immediately, CAFD was involved in its first case: that of Anthony Arblaster at the University of Manchester; and in the first few years a number of reports of enquiries and investigations were published, until the cost of printing made publication much more irregular. A number of CAFD members have become nationally known for their activity in the area of civil liberty. Steven Lukes, of Balliol College, Oxford, had a personal column for two years in *The Times Higher Educational Supplement* at the end of the seventies; and CAFD in its collective sense had its own regular column in the middle of the decade. The outstanding personality, and the one whose name has been most closely associated with the work of CAFD, is John Griffith, whose dedication and selflessness have been remarkable.

John Griffith retired from his central place in CAFD in 1982, and John Saville became chairman – with a remit which included building up CAFD on a regional basis and working for decentralisation to allow for the more speedy coming together of institutions and individuals when crises threaten. Libertarian questions will always remain central to the purposes of CAFD, but it is likely that the organisation must also expect to play a positive role in the furtherance of the democracy part of CAFD's aims; and there is in addition the need for a continued emphasis upon the unity of the different areas of higher education.

Appendix II: The Cobden Trust

Malcolm Hurwitt, Honorary Secretary, Cobden Trust

The hurly-burly of life in a pressure group active in the political field seems as far removed as it is possible to be from the traditional picture of academic ivory towers produced by the word 'research'; but, although NCCL was the parent of The Cobden Trust, the relationship of the two organisations has avoided the storms of adolescence and is stable and fruitful.

The literature produced by NCCL is designed to further its current campaigns which are usually either to change a particular law for the better or to prevent its being changed for the worse. There are neither the resources nor is there the opportunity for NCCL to consider the underlying causes of a problem, its extent and long-term effects upon society. The awareness of the need for a theoretical basis for much of its work led Martin Ennals, the then General Secretary of NCCL, and Alan Paterson, a member of its Executive Committee, to propose the founding of a trust which would undertake research and educational work in the field of civil liberties. The project was approved by the Executive Committee and the Trust was established in 1963.

When the Trust Deed had been prepared, the need to find a name for the new body became pressing; none of the possibilities suggested seemed appropriate and it was with something approaching desperation that Alan Paterson glanced out of the window of NCCL's offices at 4 Camden High Street and noticed in the road a statue of Richard Cobden. Some rapid research showed nothing in Cobden's history to be anti-libertarian and so the name was adopted. The trust was registered as a charity with the Charity Commission and was then able to take advantage of the system of '7-year covenants' under which a sum of money, given to the Trust on a regular basis, is increased by claiming from the Inland Revenue the tax which has been notionally deducted from it.

At this early period of its existence it was these covenants and single donations which provided the Trust's income to pay for its research and its administrative expenses; later they were to be used entirely to pay salaries, rent, rates and other similar items, while each project of research was to be funded by a grant given for that purpose by one or other of the large foundations, such as The Cadbury Trust, The Gulbenkian Foundation, the Sainsbury Trust and similar bodies.

The research work was difficult to develop in the early years of the Trust because Alan Paterson, who had become its Secretary, had one part-time assistant; but they undertook projects on the rights of children and on privacy. With the appointment of Christine Jackson as a full-time Research Officer, the pattern was soon established of a project being accepted as a suitable subject, the preparation of a budget, an application to a charitable foundation for a grant to cover the cost of the research and publication, and then the appointment of someone to undertake it. In the majority of cases, the researcher was an academic, who would work in frequent contact with the Research Officer. The publications ranged from legal aid, bail and tribunals, to conspiracy, duty solicitor schemes, a Bill of Rights and immigration law.

On 10 December 1972, Mr Ramsey Clark, who had been the US Attorney General under President Kennedy, gave the first Human Rights' Day Lecture at the invitation of the Trust. These lectures became an occasional series and amongst the speakers were Lord Scarman, Professor Stuart Hall and Jessica

Mitford; on one occasion the lecture was replaced by a debate between Sir Keith Joseph and Tony Benn. The lecture has not been given every year because it has not always been possible to find someone who was sufficiently well-known to attract an audience and who had something worthwhile to say about civil liberties.

From 1978 to 1981 the Trust awarded an annual price of four hundred pounds to the published work which had contributed the most to civil liberties in the previous year. The first winner was a work of academic research on plea bargaining and the last was a book on the interrogation of suspected terrorists in Northern Ireland. The funds for the prize were provided by an anonymous donor through a small private trust which was affected by the economic recession and had to reduce its commitments.

No aspect of the Trust's work has had the same level of achievement as its research. It has had a number of Race Relations Workers and Education Officers but none of them has been able to bring a major project to fruition, with the exception of the production of a teaching-pack on civil liberties for use in schools. Known as 'Rights, Responsibilities and the Law', this project was commenced by Catherine Prior and completed by Judith Edmunds, and succeeded because they secured the support of the Inner London Education Authority, whose resources of personnel, technology and influence sustained the work over a period of five years and enabled it to reach a highly successful conclusion. It did, however, illustrate how much easier it was to produce single works of research which could be under the Trust's direction than to conduct projects involving prolonged co-operation with other organisations.

With the Trust well-established, Alan Paterson retired after 10 years as a trustee and as the Honorary Secretary. The close working relationship with NCCL had been maintained by appointing as Trustees present or past members of NCCL's Executive Committee, with the single exception of a former member of the Trust's own staff. The independence of the

Trust is rigorously guarded by its insistence on its autonomy, and careful control of its activities and publications, to avoid any threat to its charitable status.

In 1981 the Trust played the leading role in purchasing freehold offices at 21–23 Tabard Street, London. The NCCL was an equal partner in the project, but, to provide a degree of continuity, the Trustees became the shareholders and directors of the company which acquired the property. In addition to providing better working conditions and a feeling of security, the new building enabled the Trust to display more efficiently its unique civil liberty library and to encourage its use by students and researchers.

Notes

Abbreviations used are as follows: *AR* = *Annual Report*; *CL* = *Civil Liberty*; *R* = *Rights*. *Civil Liberty* is the name of NCCL's first regular journal, which began to appear in 1937, three years after the formation of the Council. The format of the journal varied, at first distinguished by number, then by number and volume, and later still merely by the date of appearance. These variations explain why entries for the journal in these footnotes differ in presentation. The later copies of *Civil Liberty* were frequently single sheets; in these cases, I have not indicated pagination.

CHAPTER 1: 1934–39

1. Sylvia Scaffardi, private correspondence with Roger Cornwell.
2. Scaffardi, unpublished autobiography.
3. Already, in the first year, they included: Clem Attlee, Lascelles Abercrombie, Aneurin Bevan MP, Vera Brittain, Professor Catlin, Havelock Ellis, Lord Faringdon, Dingle Foot MP, Victor Gollancz, A. P. Herbert, Julian Huxley, C. E. M. Joad, the Earl of Kinnoull, the Rt. Hon. George Lansbury MP, Harold Laski, Kingsley Martin, A. A. Milne, H. L. Nathan MP, Henry Nevinson, the Rt. Hon. Lord Parmoor, Lord Ponsonby, J. B. Priestley, D. N. Pritt, Viscountess Rhondda, Bertrand Russell, Professor R. H. Tawney, H. G. Wells, Rebecca West.
4. Wal Hannington, *Unemployed Struggles: 1919–1936* (Lawrence & Wishart, London, 1936) p. 281.
5. Ibid., p. 282.
6. *Manchester Guardian*, 24 Feb. 1934.
7. Claud Cockburn, *In Time of Trouble* (Rupert Hart-Davies, London, 1956; rpt. 1957, Readers Union) pp. 228–9.
8. Hannington, op. cit., p. 286.
9. Ibid., p. 291.
10. Ronald Kidd, *British Liberty in Danger* (Lawrence & Wishart, London, 1940) p. 150.
11. Barry Cox, *Civil Liberties in Britain* (Harmondsworth, Penguin, 1975) p. 26.
12. Kidd, op. cit., pp. 28–9.
13. *CL*, no. 1, Apr. 1937, p. 2.
14. Ibid., p. 3.
15. Ibid., p. 1.
16. *CL*, no. 2, Autumn 1937, p. 13.
17. Ibid., p. 13.

18. *Autobiography of D. N. Pritt: Part Two: Brasshats and Bureaucrats* (Lawrence & Wishart, London, 1966) p. 59.
19. Ibid., p. 66.
20. *CL*, no. 1, Apr. 1937, p. 3.
21. *AR*, 1934, p. 15.
22. *Sunday Express*, 15 Jan. 1939.
23. *CL*, no. 4, Apr. 1939, p. 5.
24. Ibid., p. 4.
25. Ibid., p. 6.
26. *Manchester Guardian*, 3 Oct. 1934.
27. *Non-Flam Films* (NCCL, London, 1934).
28. *Manchester Guardian*, 8 Oct. 1934.
29. Cox, op. cit., p. 82.
30. Ronald Kidd, *The Harworth Colliery Strike* (NCCL, London, 1937) p. 13.
31. Ibid., p. 6.
32. *CL*, no. 2, Autumn 1937, pp. 3–4.
33. Kidd, *The Harworth Colliery Strike*, pp. 9–10.
34. Kidd, *British Liberty in Danger*, p. 59.
35. Harry Street, *Freedom, the Individual and the Law*, 5th edn (Harmondsworth, Penguin, 1982) pp. 212–13.
36. Thom Young, *Incitement to Disaffection* (Cobden Trust, London, 1976) p. 66.
37. *AR*, 1934, p. 11.
38. Kidd, *British Liberty in Danger*, p. 67.
39. Scaffardi–Cornwell correspondence.
40. Ibid.
41. E. M. Forster, 'Ronald Kidd' in *Two Cheers for Democracy* (Edward Arnold, London, 1951; rpt. Harmondsworth, Penguin, 1965) pp. 59–60.
42. Scaffardi–Cornwell correspondence.

CHAPTER 2: 1939–45

1. *CL*, no. 17, July 1940, p. 6.
2. *CL*, no. 26, June 1941, p. 4.
3. *CL*, no. 20, Nov.–Dec. 1940, p. 3.
4. Ibid., p. 3.
5. Ibid., p. 3.
6. *Civil Liberties Defended* (NCCL, London, 1941) p. 4.
7. *CL*, no. 10, Nov.–Dec. 1939, p. 8.
8. *CL*, no. 12, Feb. 1940, p. 6.
9. Ibid., p. 6.
10. Ibid., p. 6.
11. *Quarterly Case Book No. 2* (NCCL, London, 1941) p. 17.
12. *CL*, no. 15, May 1940, p. 3.

13. *CL*, no. 12, Feb. 1940, p. 3.
14. Ibid., p. 3.
15. Ibid., p. 4.
16. *CL*, no. 24, Apr. 1941, p. 9.
17. Ibid., p. 9.
18. *Civil Liberty and the Colonies* (NCCL, London, 1945) p. 14.
19. Ibid., p. 22.
20. *CL*, no. 11, Jan. 1940, p. 4.
21. Ibid., p. 4.
22. Ibid., p. 4.
23. *The Internment and Treatment of Aliens* (NCCL, London, 1941) p. 5.
24. *CL*, no. 21, Jan. 1941, p. 5.
25. *CL*, no. 18, Aug.–Sept. 1940, p. 2.
26. *The Internment and Treatment of Aliens*, p. 10.
27. Ibid., p. 11.
28. *CL*, vol. 5, no. 11, July 1945, p. 1.
29. *CL*, no. 24, Apr. 1941, p. 3.
30. *CL*, vol. 6, no. 1, Sept. 1945, p. 2.
31. *CL*, no. 3, Spring 1938, p. 2.
32. *CL*, no. 18, Aug.–Sept. 1940, p. 3.
33. *CL*, no. 22, Feb. 1941, p. 1.
34. Pritt, op. cit., p. 52.
35. Ibid., p. 55.
36. *CL*, no. 20, Nov.–Dec. 1940, p. 5.
37. *CL*, no. 24, Apr. 1941, p. 2.
38. Ibid., p. 4.
39. Ibid., p. 4.

CHAPTER 3: 1946–59

1. Pritt, op. cit., p. 113.
2. R. J. Spector, *Freedom for the Forces* (NCCL, London, n.d.).
3. Ibid., pp. 14–15.
4. *CL*, vol. 6, no. 12, Aug. 1946, p. 2.
5. *CL*, vol. 9, no. 2, Feb. 1949, p. 3.
6. *Reynolds News*, 16 Dec. 1945.
7. *CL*, vol. 6, no. 11, July 1946, p. 1.
8. *CL*, vol. 6, no. 10, June 1946, p. 2.
9. *CL*, vol. 9, no. 2, Feb. 1949, p. 4.
10. *CL*, vol. 10, no. 7, Winter 1950, p. 6.
11. Ibid., p. 7.
12. *CL*, vol. 9, no. 1, Jan. 1949, p. 2.
13. P. N. Furbank, *E. M. Forster: a Life* (OUP, Oxford, 1979) vol. 2, p. 191. The blurb,

one notes in passing, includes the following: 'Indulged, cosseted, dressed up, and shown off by his adored mother Lily, it was not surprising . . . that he should begin to tend towards homosexuality.' It is alarming that a reputable publisher should have let this nonsense slip through.

14. Ibid., p. 190.
15. *CL*, vol. 8, no. 6, June 1948, p. 2.
16. *CL*, vol. 7, no. 10, Aug. 1947, p. 4.
17. *CL*, vol. 10, no. 1, Jan. 1950, pp. 1–2.
18. *CL*, vol. 10, no. 3, Apr. 1950, p. 10.
19. *CL*, vol. 12, no. 6, Spring 1957, p. 3.
20. Ibid., p. 3.
21. *CL*, vol. 12, no. 1, p. 12.
22. *CL*, vol. 11, nos 5, 6, Summer 1951, p. 5 and 7.
23. Cox, op. cit., p. 280.
24. Ibid., p. 282.

CHAPTER 4: 1960–74

1. *CL*, Sept. 1963.
2. *AR*, 1964, p. 18.
3. *AR*, 1966, p. 15.
4. *CL*, Jan. 1966.
5. *AR*, 1969, p. 13.
6. *CL*, Oct. 1969.
7. Patricia Hewitt, *The Abuse of Power: Civil Liberties in the United Kingdom* (Martin Robertson, Oxford, 1982) p. 191.
8. *CL*, Mar.–Apr. 1971.
9. See Appendix II on the Cobden Trust.
10. Nan Berger, *The Rights of Children and Young Persons* (Cobden Trust, London, 1967) p. 18.
11. *Children Have Rights* (NCCL, London, n.d., ? 1967) p. 5.
12. Berger, op. cit., p. 20.
13. Angela Kneale, *Against Birching. Judicial Corporal Punishment in the Isle of Man* (NCCL, London, 1973) p. 78.
14. Ibid., p. 78.
15. Grattan Puxon, *On the Road* (NCCL, London, 1968) pp. 6–7.
16. *CL*, Sept. 1968.
17. *CL*, Oct. 1970.
18. *CL*, Dec. 1972, p. 2.
19. *CL*, Sept. 1968.
20. Cox, op. cit., p. 286.
21. *CL*, Aug. 1966.
22. *CL*, Oct. 1967.

23. *AR*, 1970, p. 26.
24. *The Special Powers Acts of Northern Ireland. Report of a Commission of Inquiry* (NCCL, London, 1936) p. 39.
25. Dermot Walsh, *The Use and Abuse of Emergency Legislation in Northern Ireland* (Cobden Trust, London, 1983).
26. *CL*, vol. 39, no. 7, Nov. 1973, p. 3.

CHAPTER 5: 1975–84

1. *R*, vol. 1, no. 6, July–Aug. 1977, p. 3.
2. Ibid., p. 4.
3. *R*, vol. 3, no. 2, Nov.–Dec. 1978, p. 8.
4. *R*, vol. 4, no. 4, Mar.–Apr. 1980, p. 8.
5. Stan Cohen and Laurie Taylor, *Prison Secrets* (NCCL and Radical Alternatives to Prison, London, 1978) p. 41.
6. Ibid., pp. 42–3.
7. Ibid., p. 43.
8. *The Times*, 25 Feb. 1982.
9. Ibid.
10. *R*, vol. 4, no. 2, Nov.–Dec. 1979, p. 7.
11. Ibid., p. 5.
12. *The Guardian*, 27 Oct. 1978.
13. *R*, vol. 4, no. 2, Nov.–Dec. 1979, p. 6.
14. *The Times*, 21 Nov. 1981.
15. *CL*, vol. 40, no. 6, Nov. 1974, p. 1.
16. Ibid., p. 1.
17. *R*, vol. 2, no. 3, Jan.–Feb. 1978, p. 5.
18. Ibid., p. 5.
19. *R*, vol. 7, no. 1, Spring 1983, p. 9.
20. Patricia Hewitt, *A Fair Cop* (NCCL, London, 1982) p. 12.
21. Ibid., pp. 19–20.
22. Ruth Cohen, *Whose File is it Anyway?* (NCCL, London, 1982) pp. 17–18.
23. *R*, vol. 6, no. 5, July–Sept. 1982, pp. 6–8.
24. Ibid., p. 7.
25. Ibid., p. 8.
26. Patricia Hewitt, *Privacy: the Information Gatherers* (NCCL, London, 1977).
27. *R*, vol. 2, no. 3, Jan.–Feb. 1978, p. 8.
28. Ibid., p. 8.
29. *R*, vol. 1, no. 5, May–June 1977, p. 7.
30. Ibid., p. 7.
31. James Michael, *The Politics of Secrecy* (NCCL, London, 1979) p. 48.
32. *CL*, vol. 41, no. 4, Aug. 1975, p. 1.

33. Chris Beer *et al.*, *Gay Workers: Trade Unions and the Law* (NCCL, London, 1981) p. 34.
34. Paul Crane, *Gays and the Law* (Pluto Press, London, 1982) p. 105.
35. *The Times*, 24 Apr. 1980.
36. Crane, op. cit., p. 127.
37. Ibid., p. 129.
38. *R*, vol. 7, no. 2, Summer 1983, p. 9.
39. *R*, vol. 6, no. 3, Jan.–Feb. 1982, p. 1.
40. Ann Sedley and Melissa Benn, *Sexual Harassment at Work* (NCCL, London, 1982).
41. Ibid., p. 10.
42. Ibid., p. 26.
43. *R*, vol. 6, no. 5, July–Sept. 1982, p. 1.
44. Ibid., p. 1.

Index

The index contains entries of three kinds. The first category corresponds to the titles of the sub-headings of each chapter (e.g. reluctant servicemen, prisons) and these full entries can be used as tables of contents for the relevant sections. The second category is people, and the third includes reports, committees, commissions, organisations and groups.

Some important entries in this third category will be found twice: as main, and as sub-entries. All legislation is given a main entry, whether or not it also appears as a sub-entry.